D0655134

CACTI AND
SUCCULENTS

A CONCISE GUIDE IN COLOUR

CACTI AND SUCCULENTS

by Rudolf Šubík

Illustrated by Jiřina Kaplická

TREASURE PRESS

Translated by Olga Kuthanová
First published in Great Britain in 1968 by
The Hamlyn Publishing Group Limited

This edition published in 1989 by
Treasure Press
Michelin House
81 Fulham Road
London SW3 6RB

Copyright © Artia 1968

All rights reserved. No part of this publication may be reproduced
or transmitted in any form or by any means, electronic or
mechanical, including photocopy, recording or any information
storage and retrieval system, without permission in writing from
the copyright owner.

ISBN 1 85051 380 5

Printed in Czechoslovakia by PZ Bratislava
3/02/04/51-12

Contents

9   What are succulent plants?

11   How succulent plants originated

15   The naming of cacti

19   All cacti are American in origin

23   The history and knowledge of cacti

28   Organography of cacti

39   Cacti of North America

46   Cacti of South America

52   Growing cacti

53   Location

54   Vessels and soil

55   Alkalinity of the soil

56   Watering

57   Sunlight

58   Propagation from the seed

60   Propagation from shoots and cuttings

62   Grafting

65   The cactus grower's medicine chest

66   Implements for growing cacti

67   The uses of cacti

71   The Plates

265   Index

What are succulent plants?

The latin word *succus* means juice. Plants, some of whose parts, i.e. stems, branches and leaves, stalks, flower tubes, flowers and sometimes roots, are juicy, fleshy or thick are termed succulent or thick-leaved plants. Succulence is a morphological term. Succulent plants may occur in widely varied plant families and one family may have only a few succulents. Succulent plants are not only exotic but are to be found also on the European continent, e.g. the well-known *Sempervivum* and *Sedum* which are popular house and garden plants. Succulence does not indicate any form of relationship between plants. Even such a large family of plants as *Cactaceae* has members with no succulence whatsoever (e.g. the genus *Pereskia* includes normal, leafy bushes and trees which in periods of drought limit evaporation of water by shedding their leaves). This means that a layman, who has a specific idea of what cacti look like, would not even consider these plants as belonging to the cactus group. On the other hand such plants as *Aloe* are mistakenly believed to be cacti, although they belong to the lily family which also includes both the lily-of-the-valley and the tulip. It is therefore, not easy to define the limits of succulent plants.

In general, succulents can be described as xerophilous plants in which the parts above the ground serve as reservoirs of water. Their underground parts may, but need not be succulent, as in the case of cacti which have fibrous or tuberous roots. Because of their distinctive peculiarities certain succulents, namely American cacti and many African species, attracted the attention not only of explorers and botanists but also of nature lovers and collectors.

As has already been stated, succulents have evolved in various plant families. In some they occur in such numbers that succulence may be considered a characteristic of the given family. This is true, for instance, of the cacti forming the independent family *Cactaceae*, which from the botanical viewpoint are angiospermous, dicotyledonous plants (*Chloripetaleae*). According to the system of classification the family *Cactaceae* comprises three sub-families with more than 220 genera and over 10,000 species and varieties.

Even more diversified are the other succulents. Thus, for instance, the thick-leaved *Senecio* and *Kleinia* belong to the group of composite plants such as our asters, *Haworthia*, *Gasteria* and *Aloe* belong, as already stated, to the lily family which also includes the lily-of-the valley and the tulip, *Agave* belongs to the same family as the narcissus, etc.

Like the cacti, these other succulent plants (*Agave*, *Echeveria*, *Yucca*, *Sedum*) are native to America where the two are often found growing together and where along with other xerophilous non-succulent plants, e.g. various grasses, bromeliae, and bushes, they form communities giving a characteristic appearance to whole prairies and semi-desert districts. The original home of the majority of succulent plants other than cacti is Africa; some species are also derived from parts of southern Asia such as Arabia, Iran, India and Turkey and the countries of the Near East. There is an even greater number of species of succulents than cacti.

The succulence of all these plants, including the cacti, has developed as a result of the influence of climate and habitat. These plants have had to learn to make the most economical use of water and to obtain their essential nutrients even when there is a water shortage. They are able to survive long periods of drought by retarding their life processes and, even though they appear to be dead, by storing in their tissues at least a minimum supply of water. Their odd appearance, so different from other plants, is the result of their adaptation to the conditions of their habitat; some species which have developed the greatest degree of succulence even tend to resemble decorative objects, lifeless stones or sea animals rather than living plants.

How succulent plants originated

It is believed that all succulent plants evolved from other related plants growing in a normal environment by adaptation to the changing climatic conditions of their habitat, especially the regularity and amount of rainfall. Those plants that were able to adapt to the changing conditions by increasing their succulence became the forerunners of the present extreme forms which are so excellently equipped that they are able to survive on the very threshold of death. This process of adaptation varied in every family and doubtless many plants succumbed in the struggle for survival.

Water is essential for the growth and life of all vegetation, including the succulents, which have mastered the art of economizing water. It must be kept in mind that despite their difference in form, succulents are living plants and must be provided with all that such plants need, namely air, sun and nutrients, although they are generally able to withstand much sunlight and only a minimum of water and nourishment. This does not mean, as many old cactus growers believed, that they all prefer an overabundance of sunlight and minimum of water and nourishment, rather that they only endure these spartan conditions and do so with amazing stubbornness. Their true beauty, however, is revealed when they, too, are able to live in an environment with ideal conditions.

Ancestors of the cactus family probably grew in the vast tropical forests, from which they either spread to areas where dry periods became more frequent or else gradually adapted themselves to changing climatic conditions in the areas where they were established. For this adaptation to be successful many changes in their body organs were necessary.

Thus the Pereskias, which still possess normal leaves and whose whole appearance is not very different from foliage trees, are considered the predecessors of the succulent cacti. The more cacti adapted themselves to dry environments, the more quickly did their leaves vanish because of the rapid rate of evaporation from their large surface area. The young shoots of some Opuntias have what might be termed thick leaves which they shed in maturity. In most cacti, however, the leaves are missing but in some there are still traces of these organs. Assimilation and transpiration were taken over by the green stem which stored the greatest possible amount of water in its thin tissue as a reserve supply for periods of drought.

There are three points of interest in this process of evolution. One is that in the sprout and seedling stage the plant briefly passes through the stages of development which in its predecessors took untold ages and thus it is possible to observe some of the stages of evolution although these disappear as the plant matures. This is true of the development of the seed leaves which in primitive genera are fully developed, as in the case of other plants, and in the more advanced genera appear only as traces in the first few days following germination, vanishing almost immediately. It is also true of the spines which are to be found in the seedlings of some species but soon disappear (e.g. in the genus *Lopho-phora* and some species of the genus *Astrophytum*) and of the body shape of some genera, e.g. *Echino-fossulocactus* which evolved from the same forebears as the large genus *Mamillaria*, so that young echino-fossulocactus seedlings resemble mamillarias for a number of years, by possessing tubercles which develop into ribs only on maturity.

Cacti which as a result of a long period of development in a dry environment lost their leaves (their function being taken over by the succulent stem) can no longer produce leaves, even if the climatic conditions are changed to provide an ample supply of water. Thus, for example, when epiphytic cacti occurred in damp forests they merely grew flatter and broader stems resembling leaves, thereby increasing the evaporation surface and thus adapting themselves to the new conditions.

The third point of interest is that in many instances the development to the greatest degree of succulence followed the same path and terminated in the same external form no matter in what part of the world it took place nor what plant family was concerned. It is interesting that similar external influences (semi-desert or prairie climate with long dry and hot periods) produced similar or identical forms even though the specific plants belonged to different families. An excellent example of this is the similarity between certain American cacti and African euphorbias, cacti and agaves.

Thus, some members of the genus *Cereus* resemble certain African euphorbias in their stems and sometimes also in their spines, and other species of the family *Cactaceae* have stems like those of agaves, these similarities generally being expressed in the name of the plant (e.g. *Ariocarpus agavoides*). Even more marked is the similarity between certain cacti of the genus *Astrophytum* (e.g. *A. asterias*) and the very succulent euphorbias (e.g. *Euphorbia obesa*) This convergence as well as like requirements in cultivation have made it possible to grow these plants jointly.

The main parts of this book will deal with plants that are stem succulents (in almost all the body or stem is the chief succulent part and thus the main water storage vessel) with references to plants which are sometimes termed as "the other succulents" and as a rule are native to Africa. In this case the chief succulent parts are both the stems and leaves.

The naming of cacti

The great variety of body shapes and blossoms of cacti is practically unequalled in the plant kingdom. What makes them even more interesting is that the history of man's knowledge of them is linked with the conquest of America and with the adventures of famous explorers.

Before turning to the land of their origin and their fascinating history, let us say a few words about the names of cacti and their classification. Those who wish to know and distinguish cacti must first be acquainted with their terminology.

A great many flowers are known to people by their common names. Besides this, they also have scientific, latin names, which are valid the world over. Many exotic plants such as orchids, however, have only a scientific name and the same is true of cacti and similar succulents.

Since the time of Linnaeus, i.e. for about two hundred years now, botanists throughout the world have employed the system of binomial nomenclature in which the first name designates the *genus* and the second the plant *species*. Thus if a cactus bears a label with the name *Gymnocalycium mihanovichii* it means that it belongs to the genus distinguished by the naked bud (*gymnos* = naked, *calycium* = bud) and that the given plant was named in honour of the sailor Mihanovich. This is followed by the initials of the author (the person who gave it its name). Thus if after the name of the said cactus we find the initials (Frič et Gürke) Br. et R., it means that the original authors were the globetrotter A. V. Frič who discovered and described it together with the German botanist Gürke. In 1905 the authors classified it according to the then valid Schumann system in the genus *Echinocactus*. Later, however, the Americans Britton and Rose placed it in the new genus *Gymnocalycium* according to the system they introduced in 1922. The rules of botanical nomenclature, however, do not permit new authors to change the name of the species and thus they changed only the name of the genus (*Echinocactus* was replaced by *Gymnocalycium*) and added their initials Br. et R. after the initials of the original authors in parentheses.

A species can also occur in various different permanently hereditary forms called *varieties*. Such a variety, for example, may go by the name of *Gymnocalycium mihanovichii* (Frič et Gürke) Br. et R. var. *stenogonum* Frič et Pąž. meaning that this is a variety that hereditarily differs from the type by its larger body and chiefly by its sharp and narrower ribs, which was described by Pažout after agreement with Frič. The species *Gymnocalycium mihanovichii* grows on the vast spaces of Gran Chaco and is very variable.

Besides varieties, a species may exhibit minor deviations that need not be hereditary — these are called forms. Thus, for instance, the species *Gymnocalycium mihanovichii*, which is globose, sometimes, though rarely, occurs as a cristate form, i.e. fan-shaped (*Gymnocalycium mihanovichii* forma *cristata*).

The foregoing shows that the generic, specific and other names can be derived from the characteristics of the plant, the names of people, the names of places where they are found, etc. Names indicating the genus may be masculine (ending in *-us*, e.g. *Cereus*), feminine (ending in *-a*, *-ia*, *-is*, e.g.

Opuntia, Echinopsis) or neutral (ending in *-um, -ium,* e.g. *Gymnocalycium, Aztekium*). Specific names always have the same ending as the generic name (e.g. *lanatus, lanata, lanatum* meaning wavy, or *senilis, senile,* meaning old). The same applies to the other, lower designations, i.e. variety, form, and sub-variety.

Some cacti genera may be monotypic, i.e. having only one species (e.g. *Leuchtenbergia principis*) whereas others have hundreds of species making it expedient to combine them in groups (e.g. in Gymnocalycii). Some species are constant and others are very variable, so that it is wise to indicate, along with the genus and species, the terms variety and form.

Genus, species, variety and form are terms of the lowest order which those interested in cacti will come across frequently. In the family *Cactaceae* (the Greek word *cactos* means thistle) divisions of a higher order underwent many changes since the first cacti were brought to Europe and botanists made them the subject of serious study. Today the family *Cactaceae* comprises three sub-families (*Pereskioideae, Opuntioideae* and *Cereoideae*). The commonly cultivated cacti belong to the sub-family *Cereoideae* and these will be discussed in greater detail on the following pages.

All cacti are American in origin

Cacti that occur outside America (chiefly in southern Europe and the Near East) were introduced there by man (in Australia some opuntias became the ruin of agriculture) or by birds (e.g. the spread of *Rhipsalis* in Africa and Asia thanks to its sticky fruit).

In America cacti are distributed over vast areas, particularly in warm and dry regions. Some species occur in both North and South America even in cold and rugged regions where there are severe frosts in winter. In North America some opuntias have even penetrated north of the 50th parallel, which corresponds to the latitude of Stockholm, and in South America some species grow even in the inhospitable climate of Patagonia. Throughout this vast range, however, their distribution is uneven both as regards species and concentration. The greatest concentration of cacti appears to be in the region immediately north and south of the hot zone. In the north they are most abundant in Mexico and the southern United States where they grow in such numbers that they give a characteristic appearance to whole districts, e.g. the candelabra-like Cerei *(Carnegia gigantea)* of Arizona or "The Old Man of the Desert" *(Cephalocereus senilis)* occuring in the valleys north of Mexico City. Also growing in these valleys are thousand-year-old huge globose cacti *(Echinocactus ingens)* and numerous other succulents making these areas resemble gardens purposely established for their cultivation. The cacti are also imposing in their size, for the candelabras, clumps and forests of Cerei attain a height of fifteen metres and over and the spherical species, averaging one metre in diameter and two metres in height, sometimes weigh more than one ton. *Ferocactus acanthodes* of California, with the same average diameter, reaches a height of as much as four metres. The Mexican cacti comprise many unusual genera and species, including miniatures only a few centimetres in diameter, these being the rarest.

Mexico, where the cactus is even part of the state coat-of-arms (an eagle perched on an opuntia and holding a snake in its claws) is thus the classic home of the cactus. It is here that cacti were first collected, described, and from here that they were taken to Europe in such great numbers that the government had to intervene by limiting or forbidding their export to prevent the total extermination of certain species. Cacti generally occur in the inland regions with slight rainfall where they grow along with other xerophilous prairie and desert plants. In hot, humid regions and near the coast their numbers are few and those that are found there are epiphytic* species growing chiefly on trees.

* Epiphytes are plants growing on trees or rocks to which they are attached by their roots. They are not parasites since they do not obtain food directly from the plant to which they are attached.

These regions have three main climatic seasons: the hot and humid season at the beginning of the year (February to June) when the cacti grow, the dry and hot season (July to September) when they flower and bear fruit, and the season when they rest, which corresponds to our winter and lasts from September till February. At this time the weather is cold and the temperature sometimes drops far below the freezing point, chiefly at higher elevations, without causing any damage to the cacti which prepared themselves for this during the dry season when their bodies shrivelled. The annual rainfall here is minimal (3 to 12 in.), far below the European average of 31 in., and besides that, it occurs in the form of several heavy spring rains. Summer temperatures are high (30° to 50°C) and the cold season is relatively dry.

Few cacti are found in Central America. The prevalent types are forest cacti such as the genus *Epiphyllum* and *Rhipsalis*, and various thermophilic Cerei and Melocacti.

The types growing in the vast tropical equatorial region bordering the Amazon River are limited to the epiphytic and runner Cerei. Brazil is also the home of the genera *Hatiora*, *Pfeiffera* and *Discocactus*: the drier and higher plateau in the south-east is characterized by a great number of Cerei and in the south we begin to find the typical South American cacti of the genera *Parodia*, *Brasilicactus*, *Eriocactus*, *Notocactus* and *Gymnocalycium*.

In the high mountain regions of Ecuador and

especially in Peru and Bolivia, the number of cacti begins to increase from north to south and on high mountain plateaux cacti reach as far as the snow-line, i.e. elevations of 12,000 to 15,000 feet. Found here are the high mountain Opuntias which like the Cerei have a protective covering of hair and wool. The genera *Lobivia*, *Oroya*, *Rebutia* and *Parodia* have typical high mountain members. Many unusual cacti grow in Chile, which may be termed the "lost cactus paradise" for the hard and usually dark grey-green Chilean cacti appear to be the last dying remains of a once rich cactus population of this desert land where sometimes rain does not fall for several years. This is the land of origin of most species of *Neoporteria*, *Chilenia*, *Pyrrhocactus*, *Horridocactus* and other spherical cacti besides the Cerei and Opuntias.

The majority of South American species grow in Argentina, Uruguay and Paraguay, and the greatest concentrations are found in the north-west mountain regions of Argentina and neighbouring areas in Bolivia. As regards variety and number of species and the fact that cacti here are the largest (*Trichocereus pasacana*) these territories may be considered the pendant of Mexico, the classic home of cacti. The miniature turnip-like cacti growing here — genera *Lobivia*, *Rebutia*, *Aylostera*, *Mediolobivia*, *Cylindrorebutia* — simply abound in bright magnificent flowers and variety of shapes. In this they are rivalled by members of the genera *Parodia*, *Gymnocalycium* and *Echinopsis*. Characteristic cacti of

Uruguay are the yellow-flowered Gymnocalycia, most Notocacti, some species of the miniature Fraileae and the genus *Malacocarpus*. Some genera spread to neighbouring Paraguay.

The great variety which marks the cacti is best shown, of course, in a collection which includes widely diverse types from both Americas.

It is up to the grower to find out what groups, genera or even species of cacti grow best in the conditions of his environment to succeed in acclimatizing the healthiest and most beautiful cacti. Plants grown from the seed are far better in all respects than the imported cacti which were predominant in older collections.

The history and knowledge of cacti

Man's relation to cacti is doubtless far older than the history of America. The impression made by these plants on the original inhabitants of that country must have been far greater than on modern man. Furthermore they were put to a large number of uses. Their fruit was welcome fare in times of drought and the fresh, watery inner tissues were also exploited. The Indians were well acquainted with the intoxicating effect of the juice of numerous cacti and the ancient cult of Lophophora worship, which still exists, was formerly very widespread.

The Toltecs and Aztecs, ancient people of Mexico, worshipped other species of cacti as well. This is not surprising, for these remarkable plants that resisted the onslaughts of nature were firmly bound to the land of Mexico. In Aztec relics and sculptures we find many images of the cactus, especially in religious scenes. It may even be assumed that the large, cruelly spiked cacti were used as sacrificial altars.

Such remarkable and unusual plants must have made an indelible impression on the Spanish conquistadors. As early as the first half of the sixteenth century we find references being made to these plants, chiefly the tree-like Cerei and Opuntias whose crushed joints were used by the natives to heal bone fractures. The pink-flowering "leafy" cactus *(Epiphyllum)* has also been known in Europe for some three hundred years. Nevertheless, Linnaeus knew only twenty-four species of cacti, which he classed in one genus — *Cactus*. This was in the year 1753 and it seems that up to the time of the French Revolution and the Napoleonic Wars interest in cacti was restricted only to botanists and a few collectors in aristocratic circles.

Included among the few were Dr. Karel Kunth, Dr. J. Gästner, J. M. Cels and the famous explorer Alexander Humboldt, whose fancy was caught by the cacti on his journeys in America with Aimé Bonpland.

The period between the Napoleonic Wars and the revolutionary years of 1848, the so-called Biedermayer era, marked an upsurge in the popularity of these plants. The prime collectors, however, continued to be the members of the nobility. The greatest authority, importer and lover of cacti was Prince Josef Salm-Reiferscheid-Dyck (1773 to 1869), the second after Linnaeus to establish a system of classification for cacti which was recognized up until Schumann's time. Besides other botanical works he wrote two on cacti: "Hortus Dyckensis" and "Cacteae in horto Dyckensi cultae". Other treatises on cacti were written by Dr. L. Pfeiffer, Dr. J. Engelmann, the Englishman W. J. Hocker, L. B. Reichenbach and others. Those who attained distinction as collectors were Dr. Weber, J. Ackermann, F. Schlumberger, the gardeners Selow and, above all, F. A. Haage.

Cactus growing reached the height of its popularity in the last decades before the turn of the century. This hobby spread to the ranks of the townspeople and cacti graced the window-sills of Europe along with begonias, myrtle and passion flowers. They also appeared in the villages, where to this day one may occasionally come across very old specimens, especially of *Echinopsis eyriesii* and *Epiphyllum ackermannii*. The number of importers, growers and collectors gradually increased. English and French names, which had previously predominated, were replaced by the names of German growers and authorities, headed by Prof. Dr. K. Schumann with his "Gesamtbeschreibung der Kakteen" and "Iconographia Cactearum". The German Cactus Society came into being and the names of botanists such as Prof. Dr. M. Gürke, Dr. Poselger and Dr. F. Vaupel and collectors such as E. Hesse, H. Gruson, F. Dautwitz, Hildmann and others appeared on the scene.

Following the turn of the century interest in cacti slowly waned until it was completely snuffed out by the First World War. Whereas Europe's interest was almost nil, that of America, which had paid practically no attention to these native plants, was awakened. The botanists Britton and Rose had studied the family *Cactaceae* during the war years and with the aid of the Carnegie Institute published a valuable monograph entitled "The Cactaceae" Its four volumes, published in the years 1918 to 1924, far outclassed Schumann's treatise, primarily in the modern system of classification.

However, impoverished Europe witnessed a rebirth of enthusiasm for these plants. A. V. Frič took off once again on another of his trips "to hunt cacti", this time to Mexico where he was later joined by other collectors. Europe was soon swamped with imports of bright plants whose cultivation became a world fashion. In the years 1926 to 1929 Frič discovered new high mountain cacti in South America, which were later collected by C. Backeberg, H. Blossfeld and many others. New species of *Lobivia*, *Rebutia*, *Gymnocalycium*, etc. became the vogue of the day.

At a time when millions of cacti withered in unsuitable cultures in the homes they were supposed to adorn, the botanists A. Berger, E. Werdermann,

E. Schelle and others appeared with their contributions based on newly acquired knowledge. The most significant was Berger's new trend concentrating chiefly on the evolution of cacti. The cactus growing vogue which reached its peak in the thirties also had its assets from the viewpoint of cultivation. Whereas previously collections comprised only imports, i.e. cacti grown in their land of origin, in the years following World War I there was a shift at first to seedlings grown from imported seeds and later with increasing frequency from seeds produced by European-grown plants. This was of particular significance from the viewpoint of acclimatization. At the same time new ideas as to cactus cultures were being put into practice. It had been the custom to imitate the conditions of the native habitat, namely the soil of the given locality, a dry environment and plenty of air, but gradually it was discovered that in European conditions cacti in the period of growth thrived in rich soil, shade and with an adequate quantity of water.

At the close of the 1930s Germany adopted the Britton and Rose classification system with supplements by C. Backeberg. Many collections were destroyed by the Second World War, especially in Germany, but interest in cacti remained as lively as ever. Increasing numbers of outstanding new books were published, first of all in America (Marshall and Bock: "*Cactaceae*", Craig: "*Mamillaria*") and it was America, chiefly South America, that came up with growing numbers of new discoveries as the former chance journeys of Europe's "cactus hunters" were replaced by systematic exploration of whole districts by local collectors. Collections and knowledge of cacti are being continually enlarged and augmented in Europe, Japan, America and Mexico.

A marked growth of interest in cacti has been registered chiefly in Switzerland, Germany, Austria, Holland, Belgium, England and Czechoslovakia. Not only is this borne out by the publication of large scientific works by Jacobsen (a three-volume monograph on other succulent plants entitled "Handbuch der sukkulenten Pflanzen"), Backeberg (a six-volume monograph entitled "Die Cactaceae"), and in Switzerland by H. Krainz ("Die Kakteen" issued quarterly), plus numerous books (Rauh, Buxbaum, Haage, Y. Ito) and journals, but also by the great progress in the cultivation of cacti, the number of which has been substantially increased and may be expected to increase even further. Today's cactus lovers can look forward to a great number of new species, varieties and forms which will fill in the gaps among the already known types and will thus further enlarge the already vast assortment of cacti.

Organography of cacti

Water is essential for all plants, this being true of cacti as well, even though they have learned to manage with a minimum. Not only are cacti able to absorb water very quickly, but also from very meagre sources and to store it so that it will last as long as possible. In this they are unsurpassed masters. Thus for instance, the arid north Chilean desert cacti lying freely in the sand are able to preserve a spark of life even if there is no rainfall for several years. This is the reason why all the vital organs are adapted to make the cactus drought-resistant. Chief of these are the parts above ground, namely the stem or body as it is called by cactus growers. It is usually globose or columnar to provide a maximum store of water (the stem tissues contain 90 %) and minimum evaporation surface. An exception are the flat-stemmed Opuntias and pendent Cerei, as are the epiphytic cacti of the tropical forests which had to prolong and branch or flatten their stems to adapt to the humid environment. The predecessors of the cacti were bushy and leaf-bearing Pereskias, growing and flowering much like the wild rose. The outer skin of the stem is generally thickened and often has a wax coating. The stomatol pores, necessary for the life process of every plant, are widely spaced and depressed to slow up evaporation as much as possible. The giant cacti are tall, columnar forms with close bunches of branches or widespread tree-like crowns. In age the lower parts and axial tissues of these cacti turn woody, for these giants, which can weigh as much as several tons, need a firm support.

The surface of the stem is rarely smooth. As a rule

it is ribbed or tuberculate which permits the plant to shrink in dry periods enabling it to withstand a weight loss of as much as one third the total weight. Such a drought may be of long duration and greater shrinkage is allowed by the ribs being laterally grooved or else replaced by tubercles arranged in spirals.

Roots are adapted to the shape of the cactus, the type of soil and the need to absorb as much moisture as possible during the rainy season, which usually consists of only a few downpours. They are located near the soil surface spreading out to great distances; columnar cacti are furthermore equipped with thick, round, perpendicular roots for anchorage. The roots of cacti growing in soil rich in humus form a fine, dense network. Quite a number of cacti have turnip-like roots often larger than the stem; these serve as underground stores of water and sometimes pull the plant almost entirely below the surface to better resist the pressure of the hard, furrowed earth. Sometimes the stems of prostrate cacti produce roots from the areoles on the underside and shoots from the ones on top. This is particularly true of Opuntias which can grow roots or shoots from any part of the body or even from stem cuttings and thus have an amazingly rapid rate of multiplication. They can therefore take possession of vast areas when conditions are favourable, as was the case in Australia.

Forest cerei and other epiphytic cacti often have aerial roots capable of attaching themselves to trees.

The chief vegetative centre in cacti is the crown of the plant, which is often depressed. Other generative points are scattered over the plant surface, generally in the form of areoles which are regularly spaced on the edges of the ribs or tubercles and bear spines, flowers and shoots. In some cacti (e.g. *Mamillaria*) other vegetative points besides the spine-bearing areoles at the tips of the nipple-like tubercles (mamilla) are the axils of the tubercles from which the flowers arise. The two vegetative centres, i.e. the areole and axils, may be joined by a groove (e.g. in *Coryphantha*) from which

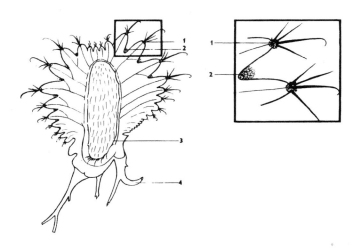

Section of cactus stem
1. areole   2. axil   3. vegetative axis   4. roots

flowers and shoots may also arise. All these points are linked by auxiliary vascular bundles with the main vascular bundle passing through the stem axis and terminating at the main vegetative point at the

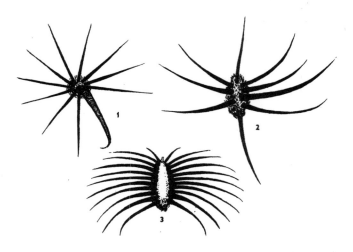

Types of spines
1. *hooked*   2. *with central spine*   3. *pectinate*

crown. These points are scattered over the plant's entire surface. Some cacti have only specific bands or points from which flowers arise. These are called cephaliums and will be referred to again later in the text.

A characteristic feature of the cacti is their

spines. These are organs that are modified leaves or shoots and not bristles, which are surface products of the cutin like the glochids, peculiar to the Opuntias, that easily break off and cause itching of

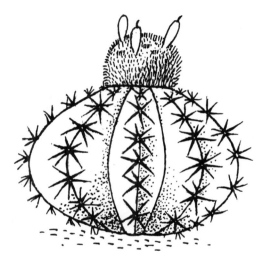

Cephalium *(genus Melocactus)*

the skin. Spines vary widely in shape, size and colour. They may be white delicate feathers (some Mamillaria), long silvery hairs as in the Old Man (*Cephalocereus senilis*), fine wool which completely conceals the stem as in other Cerei, strong spikes ten or more centimetres long that are yellow, red, brown or pure black, or large fish-hooks (some Ferocacti). Spines serve to protect the cacti from animals for whom these semi-desert plants would be a welcome source of food and drink. The wooly form are a protection against the cold of the night, not uncommon at high mountain elevations, and against the heat of the sun.

Section of Cactus flower (Marshall — Boch)

1. *petals*
2. *stigma*
3. *stamens*
4. *style*
5. *ovary*
6. *seeds*

The cacti's greatest attraction, however, is their magnificent flowers which are just as varied and colourful as the spines; bright blossoms enticing diurnal insects (sometimes even humming-birds) or the enormous white nocturnal blooms attracting the night-flying pollinators (moths and bats) with their odour — these open at dusk and last until dawn. Flowers are of varied shapes and kinds ranging from zygomorphic and cleistogamic to simple blooms, and from the tiny flowers of the Melocacti to ones measuring about forty centimetres across, the largest in the entire plant realm. The colouring, with the exception of pure blue, encompasses the hues of the spectrum and their combinations, as well as green and brown. Cacti usually flower at the beginning of the growing season, which in their native land is generally far shorter than on the Continent, but at much later times as well. In Europe some species have flowered successively from spring through summer until autumn and sometimes even in winter (e.g. some *Gymnocalycia*).

Flowers arise at the growing points and in most cases they are solitary blooms, not clusters. Often they are produced by the youngest areoles at the tip of the stem, but they also grow from other points on the sides of the stem, e.g. in some Cerei and Mamillarias. Points that bear flowers can be distinguished even before any traces of the bloom appear in that they usually sprout wool or spines to protect the bud and incipient flower. This wool later disappears. Other traits of maturity are exhibited by the Cephalocerei which at a certain stage of their growth produce so-called cephaliums, the only spots where flowers may arise. These cephaliums consist of closely set areoles which bear thick, long wool and bristles covering a certain area or part of the stem which shifts like a brush down the side of the stem as it grows. Other Cerei have similar structures through which the growing cactus pushes up after having flowered, producing new cephaliums after some years as it grows; these may thus occur at several levels and may all flower at the same time. The most perfect cephaliums however, are produced by the Melocacti. Up to a certain age these plants grow like most other cacti, forming ribs bearing areoles and spines. As they reach maturity, however, a cephalium composed of bristles and wool forms at the top and in this appear the first tiny flowers and fruits. From this time onwards the stem itself does not grow but only the cephalium, which may attain a considerable height. Unpollinated flowers wither and drop off. In cultures it is necessary to supplant the pollinator by a brush which is used to transfer the pollen from the anther to the stigma of the same or another plant of the same species (but one that has grown from a different seed) so that the seed in cross-pollinating species is pure and not hybrid. Only in self-pollinating species is this unnecessary for their flowers can produce a germinant seed by themselves. In some it is not even necessary for the bud to open (cleistogamy). Cactus growers should not resort to cross-breeding but should preserve the wild species and protect them against hybridization caused by insects.

Following pollination the ovary turns into the

fruit which shows as much diversity as the blossom. Fruits arising from flowers emerging from areoles are borne outside the plant and sometimes take a long time to ripen. Those of certain species of *Rhipsalis* have the base slightly buried in the stem at first, those from axils do not emerge until they begin to ripen, and in still other cacti the fruits remain concealed until they are fully ripe and burst. Fruits vary in kind, shape, size and colour. Some are very small whereas others are the size of plums, eggs or even oranges. They may be fleshy or dry, may burst when ripe, open in various ways, or disintegrate in a characteristic manner. The fruits of cacti are generally edible. Often they are a more long-lasting

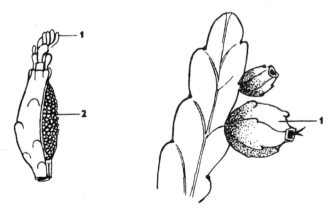

Ovary — fruit
1. remains of flower   2. seeds — fruit (genus Epiphylum)

ornament than the flower. In species that bloom continually the fruits may develop and ripen throughout the whole summer season.

Cactus seeds form in the internal cavity of the ovary. They are attached to its walls and lie in the fruit pulp. The surface of the fruit may be smooth or covered with bristles, wool or spines. Fleshy fruits are eaten by birds which thus aid in the further propagation of the plants. The seeds of ground cacti are distributed by ants. The constant and characteristic traits of cacti seeds and of the flower's reproductive organs provide botanists with a reliable means of systematic classification. They differ in shape, size and colour. Some seeds are almost microscopic, others are the size of hailstones or larger. Some germinate within a few days of planting (sometimes even while still inside the fruit), whereas others require several weeks. Some seedlings have large seed leaves (e.g. Opuntias and Cerei), which are clear evidence that these plants are dicotyledons, whereas in cacti that are higher up the evolutionary ladder and are more succulent, these leaves appear only as a trace in the earliest stages of growth and soon disappear.

Aberrations in plant forms are particularly numerous in some Cerei. These are usually the so-called monstrous forms of irregular shape or twisted like a corkscrew so that they are particularly intriguing. More frequent are stems with crowns that are not cylindrical but that grow in the shape of a fan, thus producing cristate forms. The growing point gradually turns into a growth line and the stem develops a so-called crest as if, possessing a surplus of energy, the plant desired to terminate its growth with an explosion, topping the elegant lines of the columnar stem with a huge cap. In the wild these forms are not uncommon among the columnar Cerei but they may also be found in seedlings and in plants as hard as the Mexican *Astrophytum*. Because of their unusual appearance and dense growth of spines, cristate forms were often specially collected and multiplied by grafting, a necessary procedure, for the growth of such cacti in cultures cannot otherwise be regulated.

Besides abnormal plant forms there are the ones with partial or complete absence of chlorophyll (the so-called golden cacti). These were cultivated as freaks of nature grafted on to green stock. They were either streaked (forma *picta*) or entirely yellow. A. V. Frič had a whole collection of all kinds of such golden cacti. In recent years a red form of the species *Gymnocalycium friedrichii*, apparently cultivated in Japan, has become very popular, especially in western Germany.

Cacti of North America

North American cacti are among the most widespread and best known cacti in old European collec-

39

tions established in the eighteenth and nineteenth centuries. In those days they were usually large imported specimens — colourful, spiny plants which had grown to maturity beneath the Mexican sun and were able to survive in the old and unsuitable greenhouses only thanks to their hardiness and the energy gathered and stored in their native land. Rarely did they continue to grow, but if they did, the European climate and environment, so different from that of the Mexican mountain plateaux, generally had an unfavourable effect. The new stem growth and in particular the spines that these plants produced in Europe were a far cry from the beauty they displayed in Mexico. Even at that time, however, there were already some species (and even some cultures) which proved an exception and as time passed there were more and more growers who not only succeeded in preserving these North American specimens but also in promoting their further successful growth. True acclimatization, however, was not achieved until the cultivation of cacti from seed and grafting became more widespread and until the plants thus grown produced their own seeds.

North American cacti, as has already been said, cover a vast territory, whence they spread far to the north (chiefly Opuntias) and to the south where on the Caribbean Islands and in Central America epiphytic and thermophilous cacti (primarily Cerei) are to be found side by side with South American species. In both border areas, however, there are only few cacti species and very few that are suitable for cultivation. The most widely cultivated North American species, of interest not only to the botanist but to the collector as well, come from the region along the Tropic of Cancer and in particular north of that line, in other words from central and northern Mexico, extending into the south-western United States. The most distinctive here are the flowering Yuccas and columnar Cerei and the characteristic clumps of Opuntias, supplemented, especially in Mexico, by the giant agaves and barrel-shaped Echinocacti, species that are not normally cultivated in Europe, being found only in botanical gardens, on the Riviera or in Spain where they can pass the winter under favourable climatic conditions. All these areas, along with other Mexican localities that are of great botanical value, deserve government protection as in the case of the giant "Sahuaro" cactus — *Cereus giganteus (Carnegia gigantea)* whose richest centre of distribution in the United States has been proclaimed a natural reservation. Growing in the vast reaches of Mexico and in the southern semi-desert states of the United States are a number of cacti that are practically impossible to find as they are miniature species whose stems attain a height of only a few centimetres. These are such rare plants with such a limited range of distribution (recently a new genus — *Coloradoa mesae verdae* — was discovered growing only in a single locality) that these areas should be given government protection not only in the United States but also in Mexico. The list includes such cacti as *Aztekium ritterii*, its miniature wrinkled stem covered with a sort of verdigris coating resembling the sculptures of Mexico's ancient inhabitants, several of the rare astrophytes (e.g. *Astrophytum coahuilense* and *Astrophytum asterias*) resembling objets d'art of white limestone or green nephrite, and newly discovered species such as *Ariocarpus agavoides*. Such rare specimens, unfortunately, are still being gathered by a great number of commercial collectors for sale.

The cacti of North America, however, do not comprise only the rare and difficult to cultivate specimens found in the large collections of specialized growers. Most Mexican plants are very hardy and do well even in more modest circumstances, for with a few exceptions they are not oversensitive to the alkalinity of the soil. They even include species that are practically invincible, for instance the legendary Lophophoras which have played an important part in the religious festivals of Indians for centuries and about which much has been written regarding the effects of the chemicals produced by their flesh. Other rewarding cacti are *Hamatocactus setispinus*, the well-known *Coryphantha elephantidens*, which in its habitat grows on meadows, and most members of the genus *Mamillaria*, which do so well that they can be found even on the windowsills of village homes. The chief favourites are the small, caespitose *Mamillaria prolifera* of Cuba and the variety *haitiensis*, because of their easy cultivation and propagation. Also popular is the lovely *M. elongata* and its numerous varieties, as well as the yellow-flowering *M. microhelia*, which has a slender, almost columnar stem covered with bright yellow spines. Almost identical in appearance is *M. microheliopsis*, differing only in its six to eight darker, central spines and pale carmine red blossoms.

Yellow-spined species include *M. celsiana* and *M. pringlei*, both columnar with age. White-spined species of note are *M. candida*, the juvenile form of which is a single, globose plant with a thick cover of pure white spines, and *M. geminispina* which is covered with long white spines. The popular *M. parkinsonii* grows in its native land in clusters densely covered with long white or brownish spines. Another favourite is *M. spinosissima*, a very variable species with colours ranging from glossy white, yellow, red to red-brown, so that it is possible to establish a very nice collection from this species alone. Other North American cacti that are of interest are all the species of *Echinofossulocactus*. This genus differs greatly from the others and shows marked variability; it can be assumed that in the wild hybridization is not uncommon and thus makes identification very difficult. These are relatively small, globose or cylindric cacti with a large number of wavy ribs, numbering some one hundred in *E. multicostatus*. The loveliest member of this genus is *E. zacatecasensis*, the small, flat stem with wavy ribs decorated with flat, erect spines measuring about four centimetres in length. *E. coptonogonus* has the smallest number of ribs, ten to fourteen, and the lovely *E. ochoterenaus* is distinguished by its golden-yellow spines.

Colourful is the word for all Mexican cacti, be it the stem, spines or flowers, and the fruit of many Mamillarias are bright red berries. Great variety is exhibited by the spines. Some Mamillarias have feathery spines, others have long, silky hairs, and still others spines that invite caution. These may be up to half a centimetre wide, thick, flat and red, as in *Ferocactus latispinus*, which has caused it to be dubbed "the Devil's Tongue". Great diversity also marks the flowers, the points where they emerge, their shape, size and colour, as well as their profusion. Some species bloom only after a very long period (in Europe some that attain huge dimensions never flower), but most North American cacti flower every year and specimens that bear flowers the whole summer long are not exceptional.

The size and shape of the stem of the North American cacti varies greatly, ranging from giants measuring several metres to dwarfs that are barely one centimetre in diameter. Some cacti grow singly, others form branched columns, tufts and large clumps of stems. Some Mamillarias can spread by division of the crowns into as many as one hundred heads measuring in total up to one metre across. Like most cacti, these are ribbed and in many the stem is covered with tubercles of various sizes and shapes. The skin is generally some shade of green, but many cacti are protected against the strong sun by various coatings or a different coloration of the stem.

Some cacti have very stiff stems, this being caused

not only by the skin, but also by the hard inner tissues as in Astrophytum (in Ariocarpi these are gelatinous). On the other hand, some plants have a very thin skin with delicate, juicy flesh (certain Mamillarias) or elastic flesh, making the stem seem rubbery (e.g. Lophophora).

In the cultivation of North American cacti it is necessary to keep in mind that, especially in some genera, the European climate is very different from that of their native land. Unlike the high mountain air and intense solar radiation of almost vertical rays of their habitat, Europe offers long, dark and damp winters and damper and cooler summers with long solstitial days. For that reason Mexican and particularly Californian cacti will always have more difficulty in adapting themselves to European conditions and will always remain exclusive plants, despite the exceptions that have been mentioned. On the other hand, Mexican species are in no way affected by the close, summer heat of our greenhouses as is the case in many South American cacti, which stop growing at this time requiring a summer rest period. In general, therefore, these plants will do best in a sunny, drier culture with a measured dose of nutrients, even though modern cactus growers have long corrected the opinions of old cultivators of Mexican imports, especially as regards the requirement of identical soil to the plant's habitat, fresh air and water.

North American species are particularly good specimens for demonstrating the variability and adaptability of cacti that is so much admired by man. These Mexican plants are the results of what might be termed riotous creativity on the part of nature, not so manifest in the South American cacti which remain far more uniform.

Cacti of South America

Fifty years ago botanists and cactus lovers did not know the great wealth of plants of South American origin. Among the very first cacti to be described by the Spaniard Gonzales Hernando de Ovideo y Valdez in 1547 was the "Pitahaya thistle" of Peru which is probably the local name for the common species *Cereus peruvianus*, cultivated in almost every greenhouse and cactus collection as suitable stock for the grafting of smaller and more delicate South American cacti.

Though older collections consisted mainly of North American, and above all Mexican cacti (for these were far more colourful and more easily available) growers already knew a number of species of South American origin even if they were then classed in the same genera as the North American species. Evolutionary and family ties were still unknown at that time and plants were classified according to their external appearance and habitat. The South American species were generally larger plants which were not as colourful and distinctive as the cacti of Mexico but proved to be longer lasting in Europe and to have better growth. The reason for this was that many came from regions which, particularly at certain seasons of the year, have a climate more like that of Europe and a soil that was markedly similar. This was especially true of some of today's Gymnocalycia, Notocacti and Echinopses and closely related plants imported at that time from the central and southern provinces of Argentina, Uruguay or South Brazil. These cacti rapidly acclimatized themselves to European conditions and continued to grow without deformations with far greater success than the "Mexicans". Some cacti from the Pacific coast of South America also did well in European collections, even though they developed deformations practically unknown in the inland species and those of the Atlantic seaboard.

South America was also the country of origin of the better known species of *Echinopsis*, some of which, e.g. *E. eyriesii*, *E. oxygona* and *E. tubiflora*, became so widespread in Europe in the first half of the nineteenth century that they are now common window-sill plants known even to those who otherwise have no special interest in cacti. In those days in horticultural establishments these Echinopses passed through an era of experimentation in hybridization so that the plants that are grown today are widely diversified and often multiple hybrids of the natural species. One advantage of this hybridization, however, is the complete acclimatization of these plants, sometimes coupled even with increased flower-bearing ability.

The tropical forests of Brazil are the home of the forerunners of the shrub or small tree forms with flat stem sections growing one out of the other and usually producing red flowers resembling those of the fuchsia in the winter season. These "Christmas cacti" are cultivated in horticultural establishments and are sometimes to be found covered with buds in flower shops under the generic name *Epiphyllum*. As a rule these are hybrids. This, however, is not true of a similar cactus, also Brazilian in origin, which bears brick-red blossoms at Easter time and is a natural species classified as *Schlumbergera gaertneri*.

Other cacti commonly seen on window-sills with areoles bearing red or pink flowers in summer are *Epiphyllum (Phyllocactus)* hybrids. One such species, *phylanthoides*, grows as a wild form in Venezuela even though the wild forebears of the other "leafy" cactus hybrids came chiefly from Central America and Mexico.

Almost all cacti that have become common household plants were formerly cultivated by growers and their cultivation now presents no difficulties even for those who are not cactus collectors. Every cactus grower knows that Mexican species are the most showy and remarkable whereas the South American plants are the most reliable flower bearers and require the least care.

The South American continent, which was relatively unknown country for a long time, has in recent years been investigated more thoroughly not by single collectors but by experts who were in permanent residence there, e.g. Prof. Cardenas of Cochabamba and F. Ritter. Whole areas were searched so systematically that not even small mimicking plants were overlooked. It was discovered that the distribution of genera comprising several species as well as that of monotypic genera was much larger than supposed and many new species, varieties and forms were described. Today old genera such as *Gymnocalycium*, *Copiapoa*, *Matucana* and *Parodia* have become very numerous, often comprising as many as one hundred species with a great number of varieties and forms, although not so long ago they consisted of only a small number of species. Old cactus growers remember when *Matucana* had only one species, *Matucana haynei*, with a dense cover of thin white spines and red, zygomorphic flowers. In recent years many more new and beautiful species have been added, e.g. *Matucana blancii*, the thickly spined *M. hystrix*, and the markedly variable *M. multicolor*. Of the newly described *Gymnocalycia*, worthy of note are the singularly beautiful *G. vatteri*, with only one spine in some specimens, *G. cardenasianum* with strong spines, *G. horridispinum* with pink flowers and relatively large, strong spines, and many other handsome species. Also of interest are the many new recently discovered species of *Copiapoa*. The loveliest of them all is *C. krainziana*, a small plant densely covered with long, white spines. Very different is *C. hypogaea* with its small, brown or green-brown stem, three to four centimetres in diameter and with small black spines. Two other handsome species are *C. dura* and *C. serpentisulcata*. All are from Chile. Further newly described and interesting South American cacti are the miniature species of *Neochilenia*. The small stems are connected by a thin neck with a strong, turnip-like root where water is stored for the plant's needs during the long periods of drought. These include *N. mitis* with small brown to greenish-brown stem and small spines resembling the old species *N. napina*, *N. esmeraldana*, *N. duripulpa* and *N. krausii* with thick whitish felt on the areoles. Very popular among the 'new' cacti is the genus *Sulcorebutia* of Bolivia, reminiscent of the Rebutiae with the shape of its stem, its spines and its flowers. One of the oldest known genera is *Melocactus*, whose range of distribution covers a vast area from Mexico, home of *M. oaxacensis*, through the West Indies, Venezuela, Columbia, Brazil to Peru. Flower-bearing specimens produce a felted cephalium more than ten centimetres high from which the small red flowers emerge. Other South American cacti are the large group of Cereae which frequently cover large areas. Chief of these are the genus *Haageocereus* and *Loxanthocereus* which have upright or prostrate stems thickly covered with spines ranging in colour from white, yellow, red, brown to red-brown. Most interesting of all is the discovery of a new genus — *Pygmaeocereus,* a miniature, caespitose Cereus from Peru.

Only about thirty per-cent of the territory where South American cacti grow has been investigated to date and it is therefore very likely that this continent will provide botanists and growers with many more surprises.

South America is the home of large cacti whose spines are often larger and longer than those of Mexican species *(Lobivia longispina)* but it is also the home of whole genera of dwarf cacti. The high mountain species of some Rebutias and Lobivias are practically impossible to find amongst the small bromeliae and stony ground. Some members were already known to former generations of cactus growers (e.g. the genus *Frailea*), but the world's smallest cacti (the genus *Blossfeldia*) whose stems are less than one centimetre across are a recent discovery. True miniatures are to be found in other genera as well, e.g. *Notocactus minimus, Gymnocalycium parvulum.* South American cacti sometimes grow in habitats similar to those of European plants, i.e. amidst grass, shrubs or in thinly populated forests where the soil may be rich in humus. This, of course, has its dangers, namely two: such cacti when cultivated may perish more easily than ones from the Mexican semi-desert and in Europe there is also the danger of excess alkalinity of the soil.

Most South American cacti require neutral or

slightly acid soil and greater moisture during the growing season. Growth, which in Europe begins in spring, is arrested, especially in the case of mountain species, during the hot summer months, but is renewed in late summer and some plants even produce the strongest and longest spines in autumn. The majority require less sunlight (especially in the long solstitial days) than North American cacti and also less heat. Species originating in the countries bordering the Atlantic (Argentina, Paraguay, and South Brazil) grow even if slightly shaded from the strong spring and early summer sun and even then their flowers will fully unfold, serving as proof that Europe's morning sun radiates sufficient light and heat for them to thrive. More sunlight is required by mountain species, which also need greater ventilation, and cacti growing west of the Andes, i.e. in the western parts of South America bordering the Pacific, will also need more sun but less water and less rich soil.

In general, it can be said that South American species do better in European conditions than the cacti of North America.

Growing cacti

The growing of cacti has two aspects: cultivation and collection. Although in many cases one aspect may prevail, both are equally important. The art of cultivating these plants, however, will always remain the backbone of cactus growing. A small collection of plants that thrive and flower profusely, be they the most common species, is of far greater value than a large collection of semi-mummies, even if it boasts the names of the rarest species. Thriving and flowering cacti will furthermore serve as proof that the grower has a good knowledge of their needs and does not view his hobby as mere filling in of the gaps caused by the death of various specimens so that he might pride himself on the completeness of his collection.

Location

Cacti, although they are rather hardy plants, need adequate light, heat and nourishment, at least during the growing season (which in Europe is during the summer months) for good growth, flowering and propagation. This can only be assured in a sunny site, i.e. where there is direct sunlight for at least several hours a day. Even given these conditions only the hardiest species will thrive in the home or on the window-sill, for these situations provide them with only the minimum requirements. Plants placed in a simple glass case, protecting them from dust and excessively low and varying temperatures are better off. Still greater success will be obtained if such a glass case is placed outside the window, on a balcony, terrace or in the garden where it is possible to erect a proper greenhouse, the ideal of all cactus growers. Here the plants can get adequate sunlight and heat even in the spring and autumn and may also be left throughout the winter under ideal conditions. True, during the winter months the cacti may be kept in the house or basement where the temperature does not drop below 5°C, or if necessary they may be taken out, wrapped in paper and stored in boxes in the dark, but it is far better if they can remain in light premises, for many species flower early in spring, if not in winter, and others flower and bear fruit late in the autumn.

These rules apply for the majority of cacti, with the exception of epiphytic species which prefer damp, and certain other succulents. High-mountain cacti resistant to cold, (most Lobivias, Rebutias and Parodias) thrive in the countryside and in mountain climates out in the open and without a protective cover of glass. Necessary measures should however be taken to protect them against the damp cold of continental winters.

Vessels and soil

Opinions on this matter have changed markedly in recent years. Whereas formerly cactus growers provided their plants with soil poor in humus and with a large admixture of sand and used porous, fireclay vessels, avoiding "souring" and fertilizing of the soil, today's growers use plastic or metal pots. Also becoming very widespread is hydroponic or polyhydroponic cultivation in sterile, granular matter (crushed brick, pumice, fireclay, plastics, or nylon fibres) with water, to which nutrients are added from time to time. This has caused a change in opinion as to the necessity of annually transplanting the cacti into fresh soil. Where classic porous pots are used, these are placed in peat, thereby regulating the moisture of the whole substratum.

Alkalinity of the soil

Today's cactus growers know the importance of maintaining a slightly acid or neutral soil, required chiefly by South American and some North American cacti (e.g. Echinofossulocacti, Stenocacti) and by some Mamillarias and Coryphanthas (e.g. *Coryphantha elephantidens*). In the majority of cacti alkalinity of the substratum in which the plant is cultivated should not exceed pH 5.6-pH 6.5 (pH = the degree of acidity or alkalinity of the substratum expressed in terms of the hydrogen content). The plant physiological processes are possible only at pH4−pH 7; a lower pH indicates excessive acidity, e.g. pH 2 is the acidity of vinegar, and at pH 9 plant life ceases to function for the alkalinity of the soil is too great. Some cacti, e.g. Gymnocalycia, react to increased alkalinity, which in Europe is caused chiefly by the application of alkaline water, by cessation of growth and disintegration of the roots. Previously it was mistakenly believed that this was caused by "souring" of the soil. The specimen was therefore transplanted into fresh soil which resulted in temporary improvement, the new soil being more acidic due to its greater content of humus.

Maintaining the correct alkalinity is thus very important for the cultivation of cacti. This is best determined by means of test papers. Rain water or slightly acid water from a brook is the best. Polluted river water or tap water is usually far too alkaline. The only way to combat this is to add a few drops of acid (e.g. dilute sulphuric acid) to the water.

If cacti are to be planted in the ground (this being suitable chiefly in the countryside), or freely in greenhouses, it is necessary to select a porous, unpacked soil free of organic matter and pests.

Watering

Correct application of water, governed by the season of the year and the condition of the plant, is of prime importance. In spring cacti are awakened from their winter sleep by heat and sunlight and the very careful application of water. At first the required degree of moisture is attained by light sprinkling. Only when the stem crown shows signs of life, incipient buds appear and the shrivelled stem begins to fill out, thus indicating that the roots are beginning to function, is liberal application of water commenced. It is best to supply water liberally and less frequently, only when the bottom layers have dried. If some cacti stop their growth in hot summer weather water is withheld, for they are passing through a dormant period. However, water should not be spared in the case of healthy, growing cacti, nor nutrients in plants cultivated in sterile substrata. Late summer and early autumn mark the onset of the so-called autumn growth, which should be abetted by liberal application of water. From time to time it is necessary to check the alkalinity of the soil and correct it if necessary. As the temperature drops, the amount of water is reduced and the plant is prepared for its winter rest by airing until water is withheld completely. In winter most cacti do not need to be watered at all and it does not matter if the stems shrivel slightly.

Sunlight

Sunlight is essential for the growth of cacti. Following their winter rest the plants should be slowly acclimatized to the strong spring sunlight. Some genera and species, however, prefer partial shade even in summer (forest epiphytic cacti and Gymnocalycia for example) although most North American cacti can be exposed to very strong sunlight and high temperatures. The sun is not only a source of light but also a source of heat which most cacti require in greater quantity than can be supplied by the European climate. This is therefore the main reason why these plants are placed under a transparent cover of material more permeable to ultraviolet rays than glass. Despite this, however, most cacti reach a ripe old age when cultivated in Europe. Cacti can thus be our companions for life and the majority will continue to bring pleasure to the following generation. It is impossible, and there is no need to recreate the conditions that shaped these plants, but we can protect them against nature's severity and provide them with the means for a more rapid and better growth than in the wild. How can this be achieved in each of the plant's various phases in European conditions?

Propagation from the seed

Propagation of cacti from the seed actually begins with the pollination of the flowers followed by the fruit and seed. Growing the plant from seed requires greater patience than if we purchase a grown plant. It has its advantages, however, in that a seedling grown in our environment from the start adapts itself far better and furthermore provides us with the joy of watching it grow and develop. The cactus grower thus acquires valuable knowledge which no book can give him.

The best time for the inexperienced amateur to

plant the seed is when he is able to provide the seedling with the best conditions for healthy growth and winter rest, in other words, in late spring. Artificial heat and light permits planting at any time, but the heat and light of the summer sun is the best assurance of success. The young seed requires ample heat ($20-30°C$), light and moisture. Seeds are planted on the surface of very porous sandy soil or in a sterile substratum in small dishes (each species in a separate vessel) or in larger containers divided into sections. These are covered with a plate of glass in order to maintain adequate heat and moisture. The substratum may be sterilized with steam and the seed disinfected and treated with seed dressing.

A recent method used with success is to place the seed in sterilized bottling jars which are hermetically sealed, thereby obtaining a specific microclimate eliminating the need to keep such a close watch on the seedling as in the classic method. In the latter case care must be taken that the seedling does not dry up at the beginning and later on in its development that it does not have too much moisture. Uncovered plantings may also be attacked by moulds and parasitic fungi which are difficult to eradicate. For this reason it is necessary that seedlings grown in this way be transplanted or grafted sooner than those cultivated in hermetically sealed containers.

If there is no other reason for transplanting the seedlings they are left in the original substratum until they have attained such dimensions that they crowd each other, for it is then that their growth is most rapid. When transplanting the seedling it is removed with the forked end of a piece of wood having first used its tip to make adequately spaced and deep hollows in the dish where they are to be transferred. The substratum must be slightly moist and great care must be taken not to damage the seedlings, especially their delicate roots, during this procedure. Newly transplanted seedlings should be sheltered from the sun and not watered for a time. Only after all nicks and wounds have dried is water supplied by pouring it into the dish. From then on the seedlings are only lightly sprinkled with water until they take root and begin to grow and then the healthiest and most attractive specimens are selected for further cultivation.

Propagation from shoots and cuttings

Cacti have the best natural prerequisites for vegetative propagation for many species produce side shoots themselves and in others this can be brought about by disrupting the growth centre or cutting off the head. Species with long stems are particularly well suited for such propagation since they can be easily cut into cuttings, all parts of the plant usually taking root without any difficulty and producing new individuals. Vegetative propagation permits the retention of certain plant characteristics and deviations which are otherwise non-hereditary. Further-more this method permits the immediate acquisition of larger specimens without the tedious wait, some-times several years, necessitated by propagation from the seed. It is also popular with cactus growers who do not desire new plants in greater numbers. On the other hand, however, vegetative propagation carries with it the danger of trans-mitting various defects and diseases, especially speckled virus disease, and after a time leads to the degeneration of the plant.

As in the planting of seed the best time for vegetative propagation and grafting is the growth period, i.e. summer, especially early summer. A further necessary prerequisite is adequate tem-perature and dry environment for the wounds and cut surfaces to heal and to facilitate the growth of roots; actual rooting, however, requires planting in soil and adequate moisture.

Cactus shoots and cuttings must not be too small; they must have sufficient energy to take root. Some plants produce shoots that send out roots while still attached to the parent plant e.g. Echinopsis, certain Gymnocalycia and Notocacti. Some cacti, such as Opuntias, easily root from any part of the stem and in any position. Other shoots and cuttings take root after the cut surfaces have dried, which may be a matter of days or weeks. Having grown adventi-tious roots in the air, they produce true roots within a few hours or days after being transferred to soil or other suitable medium. This method of rooting is best, for there is practically no danger of rotting and it is therefore most commonly used by cactus growers today, especially for more delicate species.

Grafting

Grafting serves not only for propagation but chiefly for speedier growth, especially in the case of seedlings of the more delicate species. Grafting can help save the healthy parts of diseased cacti and has also contributed greatly to the acclimatization of cacti. Today this method, long rejected by some cactus growers, is an inseparable part of modern cactus cultivation, especially in the propagation of miniature species and ones that are otherwise difficult to grow. On the other hand, grafting should not be used where the plant is able to grow just as well on its own. Furthermore it sometimes deprives the cactus of certain characteristic features (e.g. turnip-like root) and forces unnatural growth in length, although in most cacti the grafted specimen generally grows better and flowers more profusely.

Good stock for most grafted plants are hardy Cereus-type species and *Echinopsis*. *Pereskiopsis* can also be used for the rapid propagation of seedlings. Grafting is also an essential aid in cultivating various aberrations, monstrosities (irregular and cristate forms), or cacti without chlorophyll.

The best time for grafting is spring and early

summer, even though plants, especially seedlings, can be grafted at any time under a suitable lamp. The stock should be in the growth stage and a higher temperature is necessary for the scion to unite with the stock (except when grafting on *Eriocereus* which sometimes turns black at temperatures above 20−25°C).

The commonest method of grafting cacti is when the stock and scion are cut at right angles to the axis, the scion being placed on the former so that the vegetative axes (vascular bundles) coincide with one another as far as possible and then fastened securely to the stock by means of rubber bands. The two unite within a few hours (in the case of small seedlings, which can be grafted when they are the size of a match-head or pea), or after several days (if the scion is larger, i.e. from the size of a cherry to that of a plum or apple). It is possible to graft even larger plants, in which case it is necessary to use strong rubber bands; the process takes a longer time, and the diameter of the stock should be proportional to that of the scion. In standard size grafts (i.e. the size of a cherry or plum) it is recommended to trim the edges of the cut surface of both stock and scion into the shape of a truncated cone so that the union of the two surfaces remains intact even if the plant centres should shrink due to drying up.

In the case of runner cacti or ones with flat stems or joints, cleft or saddle grafts are used. The same method can be used for grafting cristate forms.

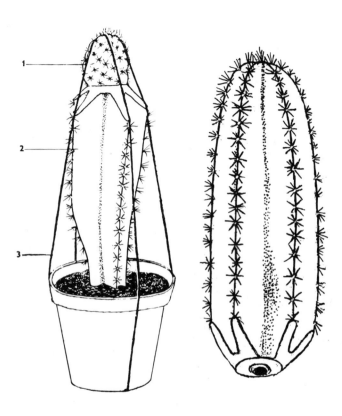

Grafting cacti

1. *graft*
2. *stock*
3. *rubber band holding the graft to the stock*

Prepared cutting

Besides being tied or secured by rubber bands, scions are often also fixed to the stock by piercing them through with long cactus spines.

Grafted plants should be placed so that water cannot get to the freshly cut surfaces and so that they are not exposed to strong sunlight until the two parts have united and the scion shows signs of growth.

The cactus grower's medicine chest

Like all living things, cacti are attacked by insect pests and diseases which the grower should know about in order to be able to treat and prevent them. Dormant cacti often suffer various defects or lose their roots. Besides poor soil the cause may be rotting of the roots or attack by pests, chiefly root mealy bug and nematodes. For this reason roots should be given special care. When transplanting it is necessary to remove all roots that are dead, non-functioning or covered with tubercles caused by nematodes, and it is best to trim even healthy roots. The plant is then put in new soil, but not until it has put out adventitious roots. For pest control roots are treated by spraying with DDT or other commercial pesticide formulations.

The stems of cacti may be attacked by rot, virus diseases, fungus, scale and mealy bugs. Diseased parts of the plant stem are cut off. Fungus attacks are treated with copper preparations and a solution of chinosol or potassium permanganate is used as disinfectant. Commercial sprays or sulphuric preparations are used to control pests such as red spider. In hotbeds and greenhouses poisoned bran is used for slugs and poisoned grain for destroying woodlice. The control of nematodes causing tubercles on the roots is very difficult. The only reliable method is high temperatures (above 50°C) plus poison.

Implements for growing cacti

Besides medicaments, the cactus grower should be equipped with various aids and implements which should be kept in good order. These include items used in the planting of seeds and cultivation of seedlings (seed dressing, disinfectants, tools for transplanting), labels, tools for grafting (long, sharp knives, rubber bands of varying strength, tweezers of various types for removing weeds and spines from the skin, tongs for grasping pots, etc. The list must also include syringes for spraying the cacti, suitable watering-cans (best with a long slender spout) or a hose with various attachments. For acidifying the water the cactus grower should have on hand a bottle of acid, a sufficiently large vessel for dealkalizing the water with peat or other suitable device for softening tap water. He should also have a supply of substratum for growing cacti without soil (fireclay, perlite, vermiculite, pumice, etc.) or suitable combination of soil, as well as a supply of suitable planting vessels (pots, tins, bowls or boxes of metal or plastic), and material for making bowls for supplying plants with water from below. A sufficient number of brushes for pollinating, test tubes to keep pollen in and containers for fruits and cleaned seeds, should also be on hand.

The uses of cacti

The uses of cacti, which at one time were many and of great importance, are nowadays overstressed in literature. Nevertheless, they deserve brief mention, for interest's sake. In the poorer regions of their growth cacti still have many uses for man. The large fruits of some Cerei, and especially those of Opuntias are a welcome contribution to the diet of the natives of Mexico where "tunas' 'and "cactus figs" are eaten fresh or preserved with sugar or else made into alcoholic drinks. They ripen in the dry season and the fruit can be harvested even when drought has caused the failure of other crops.

In America cacti often saved whole tribes from dying of hunger and thirst, the Indians sometimes travelling long distances to reach them. In some parts of Brazil spineless Opuntias are still used as nourishing fodder whereas in Australia they have run wild and in many regions have become a menace to other plants and agricultural crops.

The large branched stems of the giant cacti of southern Arizona *(Carnegia gigantea)* bear fruit even when all else has succumbed to drought. Like several other cacti they contain various alkaloids which have not yet been thoroughly investigated but are not without significance in medicine. The juice of *Selenicereus grandiflorus* for example, known for its huge flowers as the "Queen of the Night", contains a well-known glycoside used in treatment of the heart. Best known, however, are the effects of *Lophophora*, chiefly the species *L. williamsii* which is widespread in Mexico. This cactus, called "Peyotl", is a narcotic and was at one time the object of an Indian cult. It is collected to this day and the alkaloids it contains (mescalin, anhalonin and pelotin) produce colour and sound hallucinations. These cacti are completely spineless, have a small body and large turnip-like root. Much has been written about them in scientific literature and their derivatives have been the subject of much modern medical research.

The large columnar stems of the gigantic cacti of North and South America yield "wood" which is very light but tough so that in the barren, treeless areas where these cacti grow they can be used to build houses, make household utensils, or as fuel. In Mexico live Cerei, e.g. *C. marginatus*, are often planted around yards and gardens where they form thick and impenetrable hedges.

Also worthy of note is the fact that before the discovery and widespread use of the cheap aniline dyes, some species of Opuntias were used as host plants for the breeding of the insect which yielded the valuable red colouring matter cochineal. In Mexico this production reached five hundred tons annually, contributing significantly to the nation's economy.

The economic importance of cacti cultivated today throughout the world as a hobby by collectors is likewise significant if one considers the number of import firms and professional growers in Japan, the United States and in western Germany who have a prospering trade dealing exclusively in succulent plants, chiefly cacti. For us, however, the chief importance of cacti lies in the enjoyment of cultivating them and watching them grow and in the great variety of their shapes and the beauty of their flowers.

PLATES

Cacti: plate 1-67

Succulents: plate 68-96

Aporocactus flagelliformis (L.) Lem.

The cactus forms bushes consisting of stems about 1.5 cm across and 50 cm high or higher. The skin in the young plant is glossy green, later grey-green. The spines, some 15 to 20, are reddish, later brown. The flower is zygomorphic, 7 to 8 cm long, the outer petals red, the inner petals dark red with a purple tinge. The filaments are pink, the anthers yellow, the stigma pink with 5 to 7 lobes. The fruit is round, 12 to 15 mm across, red and hairy.

Habitat: Mexico near S. José del Oro, S. Bartolo on the Rio Grande.

The specific name *flagelliformis* means whip-like.

Aporocactus flagelliformis is an epiphytic plant cultivated for more than 200 years as one of the most rewarding of cacti. It is distinguished by its long and slender round stems which bear purplish-red, zygomorphic flowers, greatly resembling those of *Epiphyllum* (Christmas Cactus), early in spring — usually at the end of March. The flowers are open for three to four days. In good conditions two-year plants will already bloom profusely. Popular species are the hybrids which have a great number of flowers in a variety of hues. *Aporocactus flagelliformis* cv. "Mallisonii" is the hybrid offspring of *Aporocactus flagelliformis* and *Heliocereus speciosus*, *Aporocactus flagelliformis* cv. "Aurora" produces pale red blooms, *Aporocactus flagelliformis* cv. "Vulkan" bears scarlet flowers.

Aporocactus flagelliformis likes rich soil and adequate water, the application of which is somewhat decreased in winter. It does well grafted on Opuntia stock. Propagation by shoots is slow.

Plate 1

Astrophytum asterias (Zucc.) Lem.

The stem is flat, compressed, the crown depressed and covered with brownish-white felt, about 6 cm high, 10 to 25 cm across, skin grey-green with small white spots. The ribs, about 8, are flat and slightly rounded with a shallow groove. The areoles are from 4 to 9 mm across, grey, felted. The flowers are about 3 cm long, 6.5 cm across, broadly funnel-shaped, glossy yellow with carmine throat. The stamens reach halfway up the tube, the filaments are yellow, the anthers darker, the style, with 6 to 8 lobed stigma, is pale yellow and is taller than the stamens. The fruit is dry, brown, more than 1 cm across. The seed is large, boat-shaped and brown.

Habitat: Mexico — Tamaulipas, Nuevo Leon; USA — southern Texas.

The specific name *asterias* means covered with stars or spots.

This cactus was first discovered more than 120 years ago by Baron Karwinski. He sent specimens to St. Petersburg which were not seen again but he also sent one specimen to J. Ger. Zuccarini, then Professor at University of Munich, who in 1845 described it as *Echinocactus asterias*. This specimen also died and the species was considered to be extinct but in 1923 A. V. Frič recognized *asterias* on a visit to the botanical garden in Mexico City.

Cultivation is not difficult. During the growing period it requires light, heat and moisture, in winter light and a temperature of about 10°C. In the case of grafted plants water is supplied only in such quantities as to keep the stock from becoming too dry. Imported plants are not watered at all. It is propagated only from the seed which soon germinates at a temperature of about 25°C. Shortly after germination the seedling is grafted on hybrid Echinopsis.

Astrophytum capricorne   (Dietr.) Br. et R.

The stem is globe-shaped, later short cylindrical, up to
25 cm high, pale green, thickly covered with white flakes
which the plant sheds in part in age. The crown is covered
with densely interlaced flat, brown spines. There are
about 9 sharp-edged ribs up to 2 cm high. The areoles
with thick white felt are spaced 1.5 to 3 cm apart. The
spines, about 10, are brown to grey, regularly arranged,
flat, with stripes on the upper and underside. They are
from 3 to 7 cm long, 2 mm wide, and break off easily in
age. The flowers grow from the crown. 7 cm across, they
open in full sunlight and have a typical fragrance. They
are glossy, yellow, with carmine throat. The anthers are
cream coloured, the style is yellow with 7 to 10 lobed,
somewhat richer yellow stigma. The seed is large, boat-
shaped and chestnut.

Habitat: Northern Mexico.

The specific name *capricornis* means goat-horned; the
spines resemble curved horns.

Astrophytum capricorne, like all Astrophytes, is very
popular for its attractive appearance and large glowing
yellow flowers, which grow almost throughout the whole
summer. Collections contain several varieties and hybrids,
all of which show a marked resemblance. This cactus is
cultivated on its own roots or grafted on hybrid Echinopsis, on which it grows very well and fairly quickly
bears flowers. It requires adequate sunlight and heat, in
winter a dry environment and light.

Astrophytum myriostigma Lem.

The young plant has a low, globose stem, that becomes columnar in age, attaining a height of up to 60 cm. The skin is green with grey-white felted spots. Some varieties are so thickly covered with these spots that they completely hide the green of the skin. There are usually 5 ribs, rarely 7 to 8, measuring 4.5 cm in height. The areoles are round or elliptic with brown wool, which later disappears. The flowers arise on the crown, often several at a time, measure 4 to 6 cm in diameter and are a pale yellow colour. The style and 7 lobed stigma are yellow. The ovary is green and opens in the shape of a star; the seed is large, boat-shaped and brown.

Habitat: Northern Mexico — San Luis Potosí, elevation 7500 ft.

The specific name *myriostigma* means multispotted.

Many varieties are to be found in collections. One that is of particular interest is the four-ribbed variety *quadricostata* of Tamaulipas which bears a small yellow flower. Coahuile is the home of the taller *myriostigma*, thickly covered with grey-white scales. Comparatively rare is var. *columnaris*, which has a taller, rather narrow, almost columnar stem thickly covered with scales.

The shape and profusion of flowers which it bears throughout the whole summer make *Astrophytum myriostigma*, including all its varieties, one of the favourite Mexican cacti. It does well wherever there is adequate sunlight, heat and, in the growth period, water. In winter it requires a dry environment, light and a temperature of about 10°C. It is propagated from the seed which germinates soon at a temperature of 25°C. It need not be grafted.

Astrophytum ornatum (DC.) Web.

The stem of the young plant is globose, becoming cylindrical in age and attaining a diameter of 30 cm and height of 1 m in its native land. The skin is dark green, spotted grey-white. The 8 ribs are prominent, 5 to 10 cm high, and either straight or spiral. The areoles are 8 mm across, yellowish, felted. The spines, 5 to 11, are straight, yellow-brown to dark brown, about 3 cm long. The flowers arise on the crown, often several at a time, are pale yellow and 7 to 9 cm across. The filaments are yellow, the anthers ochre, the stigma pale yellow. The ovary is elongate, opening when ripe at the top in the shape of a star with five points. The seed is large, boat-shaped and brown.

Habitat: Mexico — Hidalgo to Queretaro.

The specific name *ornatum* means decorative.

Astrophytum ornatum, like all Astrophyta, is one of the commonest cacti in collections. It is the hardiest species of the genus *Astrophytum* although it does not flower as early as some others, e.g. *Astrophytum capricorne* or *asterias*. The many forms of this species were formerly imported to Europe in hundreds of thousands. Larger collections often contain *Astrophytum ornatum* subv. *glabrescens* and *A. ornatum* var. *mirbelli*. These characteristic varieties are often spoiled by involuntary or intentional hybridization, prompted by the endeavour to gain the greatest possible number of seeds.

Astrophytum ornatum is propagated solely from the seed which germinates with ease within a few days. The seedlings are reddish-brown. During the growing period they require a lot of sunlight and adequate water, in winter a dry environment, light and a temperature of 7° to 10°C.

Plate 5

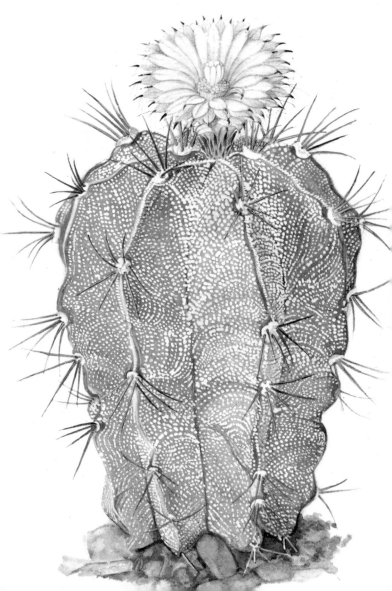

Aylostera kupperiana   (Böd.) Backbg.

Aylostera kupperiana was discovered by F. Ritter in 1931 in Bolivia near Tarija where it grows on the walls of cliffs at a height of 7500 ft. In 1932 it was described by Bödecker as *Rebutia kupperiana* in honour of Prof. Kupper of the Munich Botanical Garden.

It has a small stem about 3 cm across, globose, later columnar, coloured green, bronze with a purplish tinge in the sun. The ribs are low, spiralled. The spines have brown tips. The radial spines, up to 15, measure 5 to 8 mm in length, the central spines, 1 to 4, are 4.2 cm long and coloured dark brown. The flowers are abundant, about 4 cm across and vermilion to bright orange-red.

One of the best known species of this genus is *Aylostera fiebrigii*, a native of Bolivia, with white, bristly spines and orange flowers. The round, thickly spiniferous stem flowers profusely. Also a great favourite is *A. pseudominuscula* with round to short columnar stem, later forming clusters. The flowers are small, a rich red colour, with long slender tube. It is a native of northern Argentina, also the home of the similar species *A. deminuta*.

All species and varieties of *Aylostera* are popular small cacti cultivated like Rebutia in the sun with adequate air. In winter they require light, a dry environment and temperature of 5 to 8°C. Propagation is from the seed and from shoots.

Aztekium ritteri Böd.

The stem is flat, about 5 cm wide, 3 to 4 cm high, wrinkled, making side shoots freely in age. The colour is dull grey-green, greyish in its habitat. The crown is depressed, covered with grey-white wool. The ribs, 9 to 11, are 1 cm high and about 8 mm wide, with closely set areoles. The areoles are covered with grey-white wool with one to three grey, 3 to 4 mm-long spines, which on the bottom areoles later break off. The ribs are greatly furrowed. The flowers arise on the crown, often several at one time. Measuring 2 mm in length, they open in sunlight and are coloured a pale pink. There are few stamens; the filaments are whitish, the anthers yellow. The style and stigma are whitish-yellow and are not taller than the stamens. The fruit is small, a delicate pink colour, concealed in the wool on the crown. The seed is very small.

Habitat: Mexico, Nuevo Leon.

The generic name *aztekium* was derived from Aztec, a member of the people that founded the Mexican empire. The shape of the plant stem resembles the sculptures made by this people.

The specific name *ritteri* commemorates the well-known cactus collector F. Ritter.

Aztekium is a monotypic genus. It is a handsome and very interesting cactus. It is recommended to graft it on higher stock on which it grows and flowers very well even though it loses its characteristic features. It is generally grown grafted on *Eriocereus jusbertii*, *E. bonplandii* or *E. tortuosus*. It needs adequate heat and sunlight, in winter heat, light and a dry environment.

Brasilicactus graessneri (K. Sch.) Backbg.

Stem spherical, crown obliquely flattened, slightly depressed, about 10 cm across and 10 cm high. Colour dull green, thickly covered with yellow-brown spines. The ribs, more than 60, are tuberculate, spirally arranged, low, about 2 to 3 mm in height. The areoles are round with yellowish felt. The radial spines, about 60, are pale yellow, thin, glassy, and about 2 cm long. The 5 to 6 central spines, are stronger, brownish-yellow, up to 2 cm long. The flowers are pale green, about 2.5 cm in length. The filaments are whitish, the anthers yellow, the style whitish-green with 7 to 8 lobed stigma. The seeds are small and dark.

Habitat: Brazil, Rio Grande do Sul.

The specific name is after the well-known cactus grower Graessner of Perleberg.

Also commonly found in collections is var. *albisetus*, described by Dr. Cullman, with pale yellow-white spines and stem similar to that of the type.

The genus *Brasilicactus* was established by C. Backeberg when he separated *B. graessneri* and *haselbergii* from the genus *Notocactus* because of the completely different structure of the flower and shape of the seed.

Cultivators usually grow plants grafted on high stock of *Eriocereus jusbertii*, on which they grow rapidly and well but are not pleasing to the eye. It is better to graft seedlings on hybrid *Echinopsis*, on which they do very well, the effect being quite natural. During the growth period they require a light and warm environment with adequate water, but do not tolerate direct sunlight. In winter light and a temperature of about 10°C is best. *Brasilicactus graessneri* is propagated from the seed which has good powers of germination in a warm and damp environment.

Brasilicactus haselbergii (F. Haage) Backbg.

The stem is spherical, 12 to 15 cm across, the crown covered with short, thick woolly felt with protruding spines. The whole plant is covered with silvery-white spines that are slightly yellowed on the crown. The ribs, about 30, are divided into low tubercles. The areoles are round, about 2 mm across, with short, curly, white felt. The radial spines, some 20 or more, are sharp and bristly, yellowish in the juvenile form, later whitish, glossy, slantingly erect, about 1 cm long. The four central spines are yellowish, later white and somewhat longer than the radial spines. The flowers grow near the crown, are 1.5 cm long, short funnel form, fiery red to orange. The filaments are yellow, the anthers lemon yellow, the style yellow, the six-lobed stigma a darker colour. The ovary is lumpy, later dry, the seed small.

Habitat: Brazil — Rio Grande do Sul.

The first specimens of this species made their appearance in 1884 when three plants were brought to Europe. In 1885 they were described as *Echinocactus haselbergii* by F. Haage, an Erfurt cactus dealer and himself owner of a large collection, who was responsible for the spread of this pretty, silver-white cactus by his import to Europe of large numbers, begun in 1896. *Brasilicactus haselbergii* is a highly prized and attractive counterpart of the golden-spined *Brasilicactus graessneri*.

Cultivation is easy, the conditions being the same as for *Brasilicactus graessneri*. It is propagated from the seed.

Cephalocereus senilis (Haw.) Pfeiff.

This "old man" (senilis = old) Cereus is one of the best
known of all cacti. Even small seedlings bear the long,
wavy, silver, grey-white hair which gave the plant its
name. In its native land — Mexico — it grows in stands,
its columnar stems rising to a height of 15 m and measuring about 30 cm in diameter. Adult plants produce flowers
from a cephalium which develops at the top where the
ribs (20 to 30) change into spirally arranged tubercles, the
brown areoles of which produce a thick fleece of brown
spines, and it is from this cephalium that the pale yellow-
pink flowers emerge, followed by the fruit.

This famous "Old Man Cactus" was given a name
already in 1824. It is believed that these cacti were brought
to Europe shortly after the discovery of the New World
as a peculiarity which could not but attract the attention
of Mexico's conquerors. The famous "Old Man's" valley
— site of Mexico's largest cacti — lies only a three-days
journey by horseback north of the capital, called Tenoch-
titlan in the days of the Aztec Empire. Here the Mexican
plateau is characterized by a tropical climate, steep slopes
of deep ravines that converge in the valley of the Tulan-
cingo River whose fertile bed lies 1800 feet below the
level of the plateau. These steep slopes are covered with
the columns of these Cerei, some of which are believed
to be hundreds of years old. It is said that the oldest
Cephalocerei and *Echinocacti ingens* are as much as a
thousand years old and that they were already centuries-
old plants when Cortez set foot in Mexico.

The Old Man Cactus must be grown in a hot and sunny
greenhouse, almost without any water, in soil poor in
humus. Not until it is 6 to 8 metres high does it produce
flowers and fruit.

Cleistocactus baumannii Lem.

var. flavispinus (SD.) Ricc.

The stem is erect at first, later, due to its great length, it is prostrate, branching at the base. The shoots are bright green, up to 2 m long and 2 to 3.5 cm across. The ribs, 12 to 16, are rounded and divided by deep grooves. The areoles are elliptic, 2 to 3 mm long, covered with short wool and several longer hairs. The spines, 15 to 20, are stiff and sharp, the lower are the shortest. The flowers are zygomorphic, 6 to 7 cm long, orange to fiery-red. The flower tube is narrow and S-shaped with a slanting, approximately 1 cm-high mouth. The filaments are red, the anthers and stigma yellow to brownish. Before and after flowering the stigma and stamens are drawn inside the blossom. The fruit is round, about 1.5 cm across, and red.

Habitat: Argentina, Paraguay, Uruguay and south-east Bolivia.

Cleistocactus baumannii var. *flavispinus* is also a popular *Cereus* and no collection should be without it if space permits. Greenhouses or glassed porches are best for cultivation of the shrubs which produce side shoots freely. The vermilion, zygomorphic flowers occur on the top part of the plant throughout the whole summer. In favourable conditions flowers occur on shoots when they are about 30 cm high.

This cactus is grown in rich soil with adequate water in full sunlight. In winter water is withheld and the temperature is maintained at 8° to 10°C. It is generally propagated from the seed or from 10 to 30 cm-high shoots which after they are dry are planted in pots in soil rich in humus and cared for like the mature plant.

Plate 11

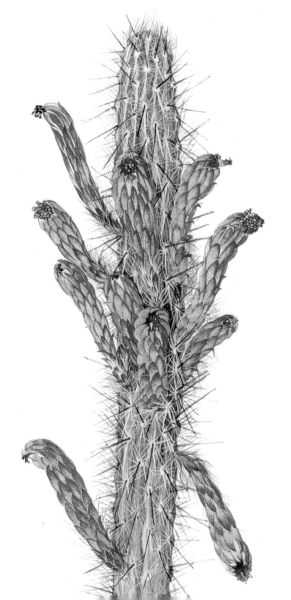

Chamaecereus silvestrii (Speg.) Br. et R.

The stem is caespitose, comprising several soft, fleshy, pale green joints 1 to 1.5 cm thick and 8 to 10 cm long. The ribs, 6 to 9, are low, tuberculate, dotted with felted areoles. The radial spines, 10 to 15, are white or darker, 1 to 2 mm long, and thin. The single central spine is greyish-white and is sometimes absent altogether. The flowers are funnel-shaped, 3 to 5 cm long and the same across, vermilion on the inside. The filaments are reddish, the anthers yellow, the 8 to 10 lobed stigma pale green to yellowish.

Habitat: North-west Argentina — Province of Tucuman.

The specific name is after the zoologist Dr. Silvester, who was the first to describe it.

Chamaecereus silvestrii is a common cactus which should not be lacking in any collection, not even in those of experienced cactus growers. It is to these so-called common types that many such cactus growers owe their first successes. In early spring the sight of dozens of these vermilion bells on slender shoots thick as a finger is truly unforgettable. It is grown with ease. During the growing period it requires light, heat and water; in winter it should be kept in the cold (a temperature of 0°C will not cause grave damage), in a light, dry environment. The soil should be rich and porous. Propagation is easy — from the joints, which when broken off and planted soon send out roots. *Chamaecereus silvestrii* does not thrive in dry and warm surroundings where it is susceptible to attacks of the red spider, which causes ugly, rust-brown spots on the plant.

Copiapoa montana Ritt.

The stem is globe-shaped in the young plant, later columnar, 5 to 10 cm across, grafted plants attaining a height of
20 cm, and makes side shoots freely at the base. The
colour is rich green, lightly tinged with brown in the sun.
The ribs, 10 to 17, are prominent, divided into large
tubercles about 7 mm high. The areoles are large and
covered with white or brown felt. The spines are straight
or slightly curved, brownish-black to black. The radial
spines, 4 to 6, are 2 cm long, the central spines, 1 to 3,
stronger and about 2 cm long as well. The flowers arise
on the crown, often several at a time, nearly hidden in the
dense wool. They are glossy, pale yellow, with broad
limb, 5.5 cm in diameter, and with a faint scent. The filaments, anthers and style are yellow, the 7 to 12 lobed
stigma darker. The ovary measures about 1 cm across,
the seed is small, black glossy.

Habitat: Chile — Taltal.

The specific name *montana* means mountainous.

The genus *Copiapoa* includes many plants that have
been well known to cactus growers for more than 120
years. Thanks to the Wintter firm, many lovely species
collected by F. Ritter have become widespread and are to
be found in numerous collections; the handsomest are
*C. alticostata, C. columna alba, C. dealbata, C. dura,
C. hypogaea, C. longistaminea. C. montana,* also comes
from F. Ritter's collection and though it is not one of the
loveliest species it is the first to flower — even 2 to 3-year-
old seedlings bear flowers throughout the whole summer;
grafted plants flower already after 2 years. The cactus is
cultivated on its own roots or grafted on stock in a sunny
spot with adequate fresh air and water. In winter it requires a light and dry environment and a temperature of
7° to 10°C. It is propagated from the seed, which has good
powers of germination, or from shoots which are grafted.

Dolichothele longimamma (DC.) Br. et R.

The plant is spherical, 8 to 15 cm high, later forming clumps. The tubercles are cylindrical, 2 to 7 cm long, 1 to 1.5 cm across at the base, green and flabby. The axils are bare or with hairs, the areoles white felted. The radial spines, 3 to 12, measuring 0.5 to 2 cm in length, are radiating, straight and erect, wnite. The central spine (sometimes 3 are present), is straight, shorter, pale brown with a black tip. The flowers occur near the crown, usually three at a time, measuring 5 to 6 cm across and up to 6 cm in length, and are coloured pale yellow. The stamens are yellow, the 5 to 8 lobed stigma yellow-brown. The fruit is almost spherical and coloured yellow-green, the seeds, measuring 1 mm, are dark brown.

Habitat: Mexico — Hidalgo.

The specific name *longimamma* means long nippled.

Dolichothele longimamma also occurs as variety *giganthothele* with 6.6 cm-long tubercles, 9.2 cm-long radial spines and a single 2.5 cm-long central spine, and variety *globosa* which is more globose. The genus *Dolichothele* was erected by Britton and Rose in 1923 from the genus *Mamilaria* because of the differing characteristics, namely the seed, which is not corky, the flower, which is large with an elongated tube, and the long tubercles. The genus *Dolichothele* comprises several, handsome yellow-flowering species greatly resembling *Dolichothele longimamma*, e.g. *D. uberiformis*, formerly classed as a variety of *D. longimamma*. It has blunt, thicker, dark green tubercles with four radial spines and no central spine.

During the growing period it requires a light and warm site and careful application of water; in winter a light and dry environment with temperature of about 10°C. It is generally propagated by dividing the clumps or from the seed, sometimes also from the tubercles.

Plate 14

Echinocactus grusonii Hildm.

This species forms large, golden-yellow spiked spherical stems about 80 cm across and 1.3 m high. In age the crown is covered with a short fleece of felt which is later shed. The plant has about 30 sharp ribs with deep grooves, dotted with large felted areoles bearing 8 to 10 straight or slightly curved radial spines measuring about 3 cm in length. The four central spines, arranged in the form of a cross, are thicker, 4 to 5 cm long, annulate, and pale yellow. The flowers emerge near the crown in several rows forming a circle. They are bell-shaped, 4 to 6 cm long, broad, 5 cm across and yellow like an egg yolk. The ovary measures about 2 cm across and is covered with white wool. The seed is small, dark, 1.5 mm long.

Habitat: Mexico — from San Luis Potosí to Hidalgo.

The specific name is in honour of H. Gruson of Magdeburg, owner of a large collection.

Echinocactus grusonii is a popular, golden spiked cactus which has always been a delight to all, even the layman. Prior to the First World War, *Echinocactus grusonii* was imported to Europe in great numbers as large adult plants which were the pride of every collection. Today this cactus is propagated from the seed. It grows very quickly in nourishing soil and is easy to cultivate. In the growing period it requires adequate application of water and warmth, but needs to be protected from direct sunlight because the crown is easily burnt. In winter it needs light and should be watered only to prevent its becoming too dry. The temperature should be between 8° and 10°C. It is propagated only from the seed which germinates quite readily.

Echinocereus pectinatus (Scheidw.) Eng.

This cactus has an erect, cylindrical stem, 10 to 15 cm high, 3 to 6 cm across with completely covered spines, and 20 to 23 straight, low ribs. The elliptic areoles, 3 mm in length, are white felted. The radial spines, 16 to 30, are pectinate, slightly curved, up to 1 cm long, white or pink. The short central spines, 2 to 6, are arranged in a single row. The flower, 6 to 8 cm long, is pale pinkish-purple inside. The filaments are pinkish-white, the anthers chrome yellow, the style taller than the stamens and with 12 to 18 lobed green stigma. The fruit is spiny, the seed dark and ovoid.

Habitat: Mexico — Guanujuato, San Luis Potosi to Chihuahua.

The term *pectinata* means pectinate or comb-like.

Echinocereus pectinatus has several interesting varieties, e.g. var. *rigidissimus*, which is 10 cm across and up to 20 cm high. The pink and pale yellow, pectinate spines are arranged in bands, the central spines are lacking. The large flowers, 6 to 7 cm large, are purplish-pink with white and green centre. Its habitat is Sonora and Arizona. Another variety *castaneus* has dense chestnut-coloured pectinate spines and large, purplish-pink flowers up to 8 cm across.

Seedlings, which grow well grafted on Echinopsis or Opuntia, are only a pale reflection of the brightly coloured, thickly spined imports. Echinocerei are frequently passed over by cactus growers for many species flower poorly in adverse conditions. They require heavier, clayey, porous soil and an adequate amount of crushed brick. Imported specimens should be watered with care. In winter it requires a light, dry environment and a temperature of 5° to 6°C. It is best propagated from the seed.

Echinocereus pulchellus (Mart.) K. Sch.

This species has simple joints which later produce shoots and form groups. The individual joints are spherical or short cylindrical, about 5 cm across and up to 10 cm high. The crown is blue-green, the lower part of the stem pale green with purplish tinge. The ribs, about 15, are straight or spiral, about 5 mm wide. The areoles are spaced up to 8 mm apart, are round or oval, about 2 mm across, covered with white flaky wool in youth, which is later shed. The spines, 3 to 5; are about 1 cm long, whitish or pale brown; those at the base of the stem break off. The pale pink flowers are about 4 cm long and the same across. The ovary is green and very lumpy, covered with small dark green flecks with white wool and 2 to 4 white or brownish bristles up to 1 cm long. The fruit is round, dry, the seed small, dark brown.

Habitat: Mexico, San Luis Potosi.

The specific name *pulchellus* means beautiful.

Frequently cultivated in collections is *E. amoenus* which differs in no major respect from the *E. pulchellus* and is therefore often mistaken for it. The flower is dark purplish-red, whereas in *E. pulchellus* it is pale pink. The spines, usually 5, are pale brown.

These plants are generally cultivated grafted on *Trichocereus spachianus*, on which they grow and flower very well. In summer they like dry heat and adequate sun, in winter a lower temperature of about 5°C, light and a dry environment.

Echinofossulocactus pentacanthus (Lem.)Br.et R.

This plant is globose, 7 to 9 cm across, later slightly columnar, pale green, with 25 to 40 acute, wavy spines. The areoles are round, about 5 mm in diameter, with 5 spines, the top three flat, 4 cm long and 2 mm wide, and the other two straight, shorter annulate at the top and 0.5 to 0.8 cm long. All are beige to meaty red. The flower is 2 cm long, has whitish petals with central purple stripes. The filaments are pale yellow, the anthers darker. The pistil is taller than the stamens and is terminated by a 6 lobed, sulphur-yellow stigma.

Habitat: Central Mexico — Hidalgo, San Luis Potosi.

The specific name *pentacanthus* means five-spined.

Echinofossulocactus is a typical genus where the differences between the individual species are so slight that it is difficult to tell them apart. One that has fairly marked characteristics, however, is *E. coptonogonus*, which has few ribs and 3 to 5 spines. *E. multicostatus* has more than 100 papery, wavy ribs and 7 to 9 spines. The handsomest is *E. zacatecasensis* with pale green stem and more than 50 ribs.

These plants are interesting Mexican cacti of moderate size. Far more decorative are the long, flat spines which are particularly marked in older, mature specimens. Cultivation is not difficult, for this species is fairly hardy and can be grown on window-sills or between windows where it bears flowers early in spring, usually already in March. It requires porous soil, ample warmth and light; in winter a light and dry environment with temperature between 8° and 10°C. It is propagated from the seed.

Echinopsis eyriesii (Turp.) Zucc.

The juvenile form of this cactus is globose, up to 20 cm across, the adult form columnar, often attaining a height of 1 m. The skin is a shining dark green. The 11 to 18 ribs are acute and prominent, with large white-felted areoles which have about 10 dark brown radial spines and 4 to 8 central spines measuring 5 mm in length. The flowers arise near the top, are white, tubular, about 10 cm across and 17 to 25 cm long. The filaments are white, the anthers pale yellow, the style green, the 12 to 13 lobed stigma a pale colour. The fruit is large and ovoid, the seed black and shiny.

Habitat: Brazil, Uruguay, Argentina.

The specific name is in honour of A. Eyries, cactus collector, who brought it to Le Havre in 1830.

Echinopsis eyriesii is a so-called "common" cactus which does well almost under any conditions and is to be found in practically every collection if not as an individual specimen then as stock for other more delicate cacti. It appears to have been the first plant on which all cactus growers began testing their ability. Experienced growers should try to locate old specimens and propagate them in order to replace the degenerate Echinopses which produce excessive shoots and have driven out the pure profusely-flowering original plants. This species should be culti-vated in heavier, rich and porous soil with adequate water and slight shade in the growing period. In winter it needs light and occasional application of water to prevent ex-cessive drying and a temperature of up to 10°C. It is easily propagated from the seed or from shoots taken from selected, healthy plants which produce few shoots and flower profusely.

Epithelantha micromeris (Eng.) Web.

A tiny, globe-shaped plant, 3.5 cm across, later slightly columnar, attaining a height of 5 cm and more, branching at the base. The crown is slightly depressed, in flower-bearing species covered with a short tuft of thick white wool. The many close ribs arranged in spiral form are divided into numerous tubercles about 1-mm-high, bearing about 20 short, 2-mm-long, radiating, white, appressed spines. The 2 to 4 central spines are white, sometimes black-tipped, 1 to 6 mm long. The flowers emerge from the newest areoles amidst the thick tuft on the crown, are white or pale pink and measure about 6 mm in diameter. The fruit is a fleshy, red berry.

Habitat: Northern Mexico and southern Texas.

The specific name *micromeris* means made up of tiny parts. *E. micromeris*, called "Mulato" by some Indian tribes, is put to the same use as *Lophophora* because Indians believe it serves to widen the eyes so that they might see witches, to prolong life and to increase the speed of fast runners.

Epithelantha micromeris is cultivated with ease. During the growing period it requires plenty of sun and heat, imported plants only a slight application of water; in winter a dry, light environment with temperature between 5° and 10°C, and heavier, clayey, porous soil. It is easily propagated from the shoots which are detached from older plants and after 14 days planted in a bowl or small pot with light sandy soil. The seedlings are delicate and therefore are grafted on hybrid Echinopsis soon after sprouting.

Eriocactus leninghausii   (Hge. jr.) Backbg.

A columnar cactus, growing to a height of 1 m in its native habitat. It is 10 cm across and makes side shoots freely at the base in age. The skin is green at the crown, dull to corky at the base. The ribs, some 30 or more, are comparatively narrow, 5 to 7 mm high, slightly wavy. The oblique crown is covered with spines and wool which is later shed. The 15 to 20 radial spines are 0.5 to 1 cm long, radiating. The central spines, 3 to 4, are stronger, darker, up to 4 cm long, flexible, straight or slightly curved. The flowers emerge on the crown, often several at a time; they are lemon yellow, shiny and broad, up to 6 cm across. The filaments and anthers are yellow, the style is pale yellow and terminates in a 9 to 14 lobed stigma. The ovary is dry and covered with whitish wool and brown spines. The seed is small.

Habitat: Brazil — Rio Grande do Sul.

Eriocactus leninghausii was introduced into Europe in the second half of the 19th century and described by F. Haage as *Pilocereus leninghausii*. In the same year, 1895, *Prof. K. Schumann* described it as *Echinocactus leninghausii*. A. Berger classified it in the genus *Notocactus*, from which it was separated in 1942 by C. Backeberg for its columnar shape and yellow stigma, that of other Notocacti being purplish-violet, and classified in the genus *Eriocactus*.

This cactus is cultivated without difficulty. During the growth period it needs a warmer environment with light and adequate water; in winter light and a temperature of about 10°C. It is propagated with comparative ease from the seed, rarely from shoots.

Eriocereus martinii (Lab.) Ricc.

This erect cactus grows to a height of 2 m; it branches at the base, producing dark green shoots 2 to 2.5 cm thick. The 5 to 6 ribs merge in age. The areoles are round, 3 mm across, with grey wool. The radial spines, 5 to 6, are red, the central spine, 2 to 3 cm long, pale brown or white, with dark underside and tip. The flowers are 20 cm long or longer, funnelform, 17 to 18 cm across, pure white. The stamens are grouped in a dense cluster reaching midway up the flower tube. The anthers are pale yellow. The pistil, taller than the stamens, terminates in a pale 14-lobed stigma. The fruit is ovoid, 5 to 6 cm long, 4.5 cm wide, scaly, red. It splits down its length. The seed is large, black.

Habitat: Argentina, northern Chaco.

The genus *Eriocereus* grows in clumps in its native habitat, forming mostly thickets of weak branches with few ribs. The flowers are large and night-blooming. This cactus is generally grown in greenhouses or glassed porches and is cultivated as excellent stock. The genus *Eriocereus* includes, among others, the variety *guelichii* which has three- to four-sided branches requiring support. New spines are black-red. *E. pomanensis* and *E. tortuosus* are very similar, the spines measuring up to 2 cm in length. *E. jusbertii* is one of the best known species with more erect branches up to 2 m long, white, perfumed flowers 20 cm long. It is a very desirable stock with cactus growers. It was believed to be an intergeneric hybrid with *Echinopsis eyriesii* the pollen of which is used to fertilize *E. jusbertii* and has a germinant seed. Seedlings of this species are far better as stock than propagated cuttings. All species of *Eriocereus* do best in greenhouses and their flowers are hardly less profuse than those of the Queen of the Night. They prefer rich soil, sun and adequate moisture; in winter, light and a temperature of 8°C.

Plate 22

Eriosyce ceratistes (Otto) Br. et R.

The stem is spherical, 50 cm across and even larger. The crown is felted, very spiny, pale green, dull. The 30 or more ribs are acute, 2 to 3 cm high, with large, white-felted areoles bearing 18 to 20 spines. The radial spines are difficult to distinguish from the central spines; they are straight or slightly curved, bulbous at the base, honey-yellow to brownish-black, about 3 cm long. The flowers are bell- or funnel-shaped, 4 to 5 cm long, about 3 cm across and carmine. The fruit, 4 cm long and 3 cm across, is spiny and covered with white wool. The seed is black and measures 2.5 mm.

Habitat: Chile — Santiago de Chile, elevation 600 to 7500 ft.

The specific name *ceratistes* has been known to cactus growers since 1837 and for many years it was a rare Chilean cactus. Recently, however, a detailed investigation of Chilean territory revealed the existence of several varieties or rather local forms. This is borne out by the varieties described and named by Backeberg after their location, e.g. *Eriosyce ceratistes*, var. *combarbalensis, coquibensis, jorgensis, mollesensis, vallenarensis* and *zorillaensis*. The specimens from Ritter's collection that are the most popular with cactus growers are *E. ausseliana*, *E. lampampaensis* and *E. lhotzkyanae*, classed by Krainz and Ritter as species.

Cultivation is not difficult. In collections seedlings of this cactus are generally grafted on hybrid Echinopsis or short stock of *Eriocereus jusbertii*. It requires sun and fresh air, during the growing period adequate water, in winter light, a dry environment and temperature of 6° to 10°C.

Plate 23

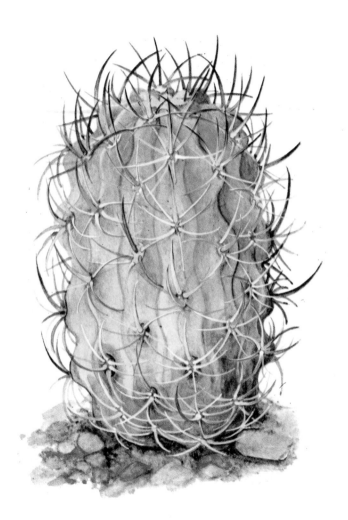

Espostoa lanata (HBK) Br. et R.

An interesting arborescent cactus with a low stem 2 to 4 m high. The individual branches are 1 m long, 15 cm thick, with twenty low ribs covered with thick, white wool. Besides the wool, the areoles, bear numerous acicular varicoloured spines. The flowers, white with pink inside, are about 6 cm across, and emerge from the pseudocephalium which forms on the upper part of the stem only in flower-bearing plants.

Habitat: Northern Peru and southern Ecuador.

The specific name *lanata* means wavy.

Espostoa lanata, together with Oreocerei and *Cephalocereus senilis* belongs among the showpieces of small and large collections. It is especially decorative in greenhouses or glassed porches where it attains larger dimensions. It does well unpotted, soon reaching flower-bearing proportions. The cristate forms of this species are among the most popular.

During the growing period it requires adequate sun, heat and rich soil. The usual form of cultivation is either the seedling or shoots grafted on strong stock of the genus *Piptanthocereus peruvianus, jamacaru* or *dayamii* on which the thick wool and spines, so beautifully coloured in some forms and varieties, are particularly striking. Just as satisfactory is the cultivation of plants on their own roots grown from the seed, which has good powers of germination in a warm and moist environment. The seed is planted on the surface of sandy soil in a flowerpot or bowl in spring or early summer.

Plate 24

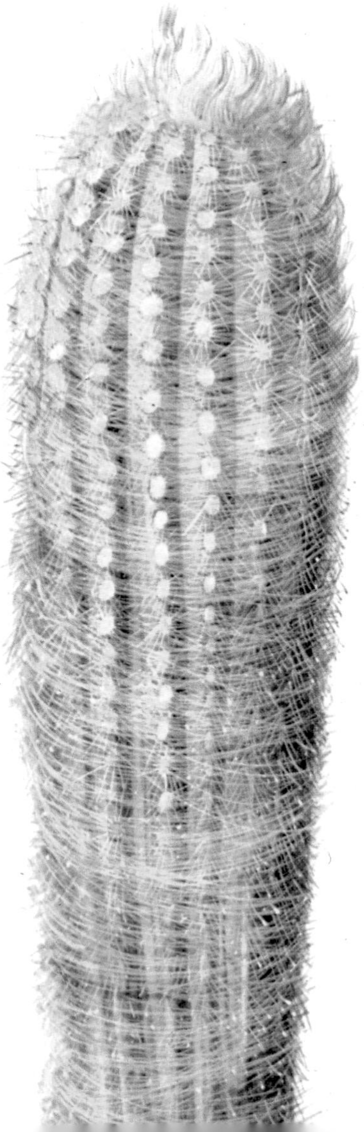

Gymnocalycium baldianum Speg.

The stem is spherical, somewhat flattened, about 7 cm in diameter, blue-grey. The 9 to 10 broad ribs are divided by deep grooves into tubercles with deep-set areoles bearing 5 to 7 thin radial spines that are straight or curved toward the stem. The spines are grey, tinged with red at the base. The flowers emerge on the crown, measure 3 to 4 cm in length and the same across, open wide in sunlight and are coloured purplish-red, sometimes pinkish-purple. The stamens are purple, the anthers and 6 lobed stigma whitish-yellow. The ovary is long and splits down its length.

Habitat: Argentina, Catamarca Province.

Gymnocalycium baldianum received its name from the Argentine botanist Spegazzini in 1905 but remained long unknown in collections. It was not till the thirties that A. V. Frič, who called it *Gymnocalycium venturi*, brought it to Europe from the mountains near Catamarca. Almost at the same time Prof. Werdermann described in Germany a slightly different variety bearing red flowers as *Gymnocalycium sanguiniflorum*. Since most of the then known cacti bore white, pink or yellow flowers the dark, blood-red blossoms of *Gymnocalycium baldianum* caused a sensation among cactus growers.

Shortly after Backeberg discovered another cactus with wine-red flowers appearing later and less frequently, which he named *Gymnocalycium oenanthemum*. Though other red-blooming species were discovered later as well, *Gymnocalycium baldianum* has remained the favourite.

Cultivation is not difficult, though the plant does poorly if exposed to constant drought and direct sunlight. In winter it requires a dry and cold environment. It is best propagated from the seed.

Gymnocalycium denudatum (Lk. et Otto) Pfeiff.

The stem is spherical, becoming slightly columnar in age, 5 to 15 cm across, up to 20 cm high, branching from the base in age. The skin is a shining pale green. The 5 to 8 ribs are divided by faint cross grooves. The large areoles are covered with short, pale brown, later grey wool. The spines are pale brown, later grey, appressed, slightly curved — there are usually 5, measuring 1 to 1.5 mm in length. The flowers arise near the crown, are pure white, sometimes tinged with pink. The ovary is short, broad, pale green, scantily covered with scales, and splitting down its length when ripe. The seed is large and black, with good powers of germination.

Habitat: Southern Brazil or Uruguay.

The specific name *denudatum* means naked.

Often called the "spider cactus", *Gymnocalycium denudatum* has been known for more than a hundred years and is one of the basic specimens of every collection. The original plant was shipped in 1825 by Sellow from southern Brazil or Uruguay to Berlin, where three years after it was named *Echinocactus denudatus*. In 1845 Dr. Pfeiffer transferred it to the genus *Gymnocalycium*. Today collectors grow two types of *Gymnocalycium denudatum* — the so-called German type described above and a second smaller type brought to Europe from southern Brazil by C. Backeberg.

Both types are very handsome, flower profusely throughout the summer and require little care. They must however be shielded from direct sunlight. They are cultivated in rich, porous soil and supplied with adequate water during the growing period. They are propagated from the seed or from shoots detached from older plants.

Plate 26

Gymnocalycium denudatum cv. Jan Šuba Paž.

This new hybrid species is a cross between the white-flowering *Gymnocalycium denudatum* brought from Rio Grande do Sul by C. Backeberg and red-flowering *Gymnocalycium baldianum*, which markedly differ from one another not only in the colour of their blossoms but also in the shape of the stem. Attempts at cross breeding remained without success for a long time until after several years one of the parent plants produced an ovary with large red seeds which germinated successfully. The large seedlings resembled the parent plant *Gymnocalycium denudatum* and in the third year bore large pink flowers which produced large ovaries with germinant seeds without artificial pollination. The following generation showed uniform characteristics, all except the flowers, which ranged in colour from white, to pink to carmine red. This and all ensuing generations continued to produce ovaries with germinant seeds. The outcome of the selection applied in the process is the present species with large pinkish-red blossoms, the plant's greatest adornment. Further good features of the new species are self-pollination and resistance to disease and pests, which make this a popular specimen with those who like flowering cacti.

It is cultivated in good, nourishing and porous soil with adequate application of water in the growing period. It should be kept away from direct sunlight. It is easily propagated from the seed.

Plate 27

Gymnocalycium gibbosum (Haw.) Pfeiff.

In youth the plant is spherical, up to 15 cm across, becoming columnar in age and reaching a height of 20 cm. The skin is blue-green, grey-green in age, corky at the base. The crown is spineless. The 12 to 19 ribs are sharply demarcated and tuberculate, the tubercles 1.5 cm high. The areoles are large, round or elliptic with grey-brown felt. The spines are straight or slightly curved, pale brown, later grey. The 7 to 10 radial spines are slantingly erect, the 1 to 2 central spines are awl-shaped. The flowers are 6 cm long, funnelform, whitish; the filaments are white, the anthers pale yellow. The 12 lobed stigma white, the ovary ovoid, the seeds dark.

Habitat: Southern Argentina.

The specific name *gibbosum* means lumpy.

Gymnocalycium gibbosum has been known under the generic name *Gymnocalycium* for more than 120 years. It is widespread in Argentina and literature cites numerous varieties. Best known is var. *nigrum* which is blackish-green with 6 to 7 strong black spines; var. *nobilis*, about 20 cm in diameter and with approximately 20 whitish spines with ruby base, is perhaps the loveliest and rarest of all. Less widespread are the varieties *ferox, fennellii* and *caespitosum* comprising several forms. They are all pretty and rewarding plants, resistant to cold, so that they will grow even in adverse conditions. They grow very slowly, however, and are therefore generally cultivated as grafts in order to speed up growth and flower bearing, though even small, 3 to 4-year-old seedlings produce large white blossoms. These are self-pollinating, as a rule, and thus exclude the danger of hybridization.

Gymnocalycium friedrichii   (Werd.) Paž.

The fairly small stem with eight acute ribs attains a height
and diameter of only 5 to 6 cm. The skin is rough textured
and brownish-red, in some forms sometimes dark purple.
In youth this cactus is distinguished by pale stripes on
the sides of the ribs, shining, wet-like skin and white
wooly areoles bearing fragile yellowish spines; it is a
characteristic plant resembling polished agate. Even
young plants have naked, scaly flower buds throughout
the summer which develop into pale pink blossoms with
slender blue-green tubes. The fruit is red, dehiscent, the
seeds brown, $\frac{3}{4}$ mm large, with rough, typical testa.
Seedlings, sprouting best after two years, grow slowly at
first and resemble pale, speckled stars at this stage.

Various varieties and forms of this species are widely
distributed, like the related species *G. mihanovichii*, in
Gran Chaco, where they grow in sparse woods among
grass and ground palms.

G. mihanovichii and *G. friedrichii* are the best known
and commonest species of this genus. They tolerate the
hot and dry climate of the subtropical to tropical rain
forests with their periodic downpours. They often do well
even in forest soil rich in humus. They thrive best in
hotbeds or greenhouses where the heat and occasional
liberal application of water provide the most suitable
conditions for their growth. In winter they will do without any water at a temperature of about 10°C. Cacti
cultivated on window-sills should always be grafted for
only thus is there assurance of luxuriant growth and
proliferous flowers. Plants often bear buds, flowers and
fruit at the same time from early spring until late autumn.

Gymnocalycium multiflorum (Hook.) Br. et R.

Gymnocalycia are widely distributed throughout South America, but the greatest number of species are to be found in the foothills of the Andes, chiefly in the hilly country of Central Argentina near Cordoba. This is also the habitat of the species *G. multiflorum* of the group *Microsemineae*. This species was first described more than a hundred years ago.

The body is 9 cm high, about 12 cm across, often forming whole groups of stems; it is pale green, globose. The ribs, 10 to 15, have pronounced tubercles with areoles bearing strong, yellowish spines, all radial. The lovely flowers, up to 4 cm large, are campanulate, white to pinkish, with short tube. The ovary is large, splitting down its length and containing large black seeds.

Even in Schumann's day two other pretty varieties were known besides the type, namely *G. multiflorum* var. *albispinum* and var. *parisiense*. The former differs from the type by its blue-green skin and thick, about 3 cm long, somewhat flattened, whitish to pure white spines, numbering about ten to each areole. In age it is cylindrical. The second variety bears a greater number of whitish, interlaced and variously curved spines tinged with red at the base.

There appear to be many forms of *G. multiflorum* as is evidenced by the great variability of older, imported specimens. In their habitat, however, their number seems to have been greatly limited by the increasing cultivation of the land and spread of civilization in general. During the last war, however, E. Vatter still found some beautiful specimens, one of which is even said to have borne red flowers.

Gymnocalycium quehlianum (Hge.jr.) Berg.

In youth the body is flattened, globose, about 7 cm across, 3.5 cm high, later it becomes cylindrical, attaining a height of 15 cm. The skin is a dull grey-green, brownish-green in the sun. The ribs are broken into tubercles separated by sharp cross grooves. The areoles are oval, about 2 mm across, with whitish felt. The radial spines, 5, are about 5 mm long, brown, grey-brown to brownish-red at the base. The flowers emerge on the crown, several at a time as a rule. They are 6 to 7 cm long, funnel-shaped, whitish, with carmine centre. The seed is small, brown, boat-shaped.

Habitat: Argentina — Cordoba.

Gymnocalycium quehlianum does well on its own roots but requires porous, slightly acidic soil. Watering, which generally alkalinizes the soil, causes the plant, like all Gymnocalycia, to lose its roots. The best method of cultivation is a semi-hydroponic culture in sterile and porous fine crushed brick or stone, the required nutrients being supplied by watering. These cacti do not tolerate excessive sunlight and heat combined with a dry atmosphere. They do well in partial shade to which they are accustomed in the grassy environment of their habitat — the mountains of Cordoba in Central Argentina.

Found there are also local varieties differing from the type in the colour of the spines — yellow in var. *flavispina* and whitish in var. *albispinum,* in the colour of the flowers — pinkish in var. *zantnerianum,* and in the shape of the ribs — var. *rolfianum.* Miniature *gymnocalycia,* e.g. *G. parvulum, G. ragonesii* and *G. asterium* var. *minimum,* also belong to the same group. They are grown chiefly from seed.

 Plate 31

Hamatocactus setispinus (Eng.) Br. et R.

Globose or cylindrical, dark green, about 15 cm high, 10 cm or more across, with 13 or more sharp, pronounced ribs. Areoles oval with short white felt. Radial spines, 12 to 15, radiating, oblique, thin, dark brown or white, the bottom ones 5 mm long. The one central spine, 2 to 4 cm long, is erect, hooked, dark brown with pale tip. The flowers emerge near the crown; they are 7 cm long, with broad limb, yellow inside with carmine throat. The filaments and anthers are yellow, as is the style yellow, which terminates in 5 to 8 lobed stigma. The fruit is round, up to 1.5 cm across, and red. The seed is round, 1.5 mm across, and black.

Habitat: Southern Texas and northern Mexico.

The specific name *setispinus* means bristly.

Sometimes found in collections are the varieties *H. setispinus* var. *cachetianus* and var. *orcuttii*. All are hardy and rewarding plants popular with growers. They are heartily recommended for cultivation and should not be missing from any collection. These cacti are fairly small plants with decorative spines and large, scented, yellow, red-throated flowers; even small seedlings bloom continually throughout the summer. The round, red fruits are also attractive. This species does well on its own roots in a warm, sunny spot with adequate watering. During the growing period it must not become over-dry and lose its roots for it takes a long time to produce new roots and resume its growth. It requires rich, porous soil. It is grown from the seed which has good powers of germination. Even 2 to 3-year-old seedlings will generally bear flowers.

Islaya flavida

Ritt. (Islaya grandiflorens Rauh et Backbg.)

This rare plant has not been fully described to date and F. Ritter, who discovered it, provided only a brief description which indicates that it has pale yellow spines with darker tips (*flavidus* — yellowish). Backeberg believed it to be identical with the species *I. grandiflorens* with a stem measuring about 10 cm and spines corresponding to Ritter's description. Even small seedlings bear flowers which are about 4 cm broad and yellow inside. The habitat is southern Peru. *Islaya flavida* is one of the many new plants which have recently been added to this genus.

More detailed investigation has shown that these cacti growing in the arid deserts on the Pacific coast of southern Peru to northern Chile are so different that they require the classification in an independent genus. The red, thick-skinned fruits are hollow and the seeds, filling only the upper part of the fruit, are encased in a special sac. These black seeds remain dormant for a long time, which is apparently connected with the long periods of drought in the plant's habitat.

Islayas grow in territory where there is no rainfall, often for years at a time, so that the cacti lie in the sandy or stony desert without any roots whatsoever, remaining alive only thanks to the mists from the nearby sea. Although imported plants last only for a short time, seedlings that have been grown in Europe are fairly hardy and often flower even when young, bearing yellow or reddish blossoms, especially if grafted on short stock. As a rule these cacti are small plants which grow very slowly in the wild. They are distinguished by a rich coat of wool on the crown, typical spines and fairly large, yellow-red flowers.

Leuchtenbergia principis Hook.

The body is simple, branching from the base in age. It attains a height of 50 cm, in its habitat up to 70 cm. The plant is distinguished by pronounced triangular tubercles up to 12 cm in length which later gradually turn grey, then brown and finally die and break off leaving scars on the plant body. The spines are soft, papery, yellow-brown; the radial spines, 6 to 14, are variously curved, the one or two central spines are generally straight or slightly curved, and up to 15 cm long. The flowers arise on the top of the youngest tubercles on the inner side of the areole. They are up to 8 cm long, funnel-shaped glossy and yellow-green. The tips of the petals are brown, sometimes terminating in a small, somewhat broader spine. The fruit is spindle-shaped, covered with small, dry scales. The seed is fairly large, dark brown and finely furrowed.

Habitat: San Luis Potosi, Hidalgo, elevation 4800 to 6000 ft.

The specific name *principis* means princely.

Its remarkable growth and beautiful flowers make this Mexican species a truly unique specimen among cacti. In its habitat it grows scattered over fairly large areas. *Leuchtenbergia* grows and flowers well in Europe, be it cultivated as an imported plant or grafted as a seedling which bears flowers after 5 to 6 years. It is a hardy plant which does well if kept in a warm and light place. During the growing period it does not tolerate direct sunlight and therefore should be placed in partial shade. In winter it requires a cool, dry atmosphere.

Plate 34

Lobivia famatimensis (Speg.) Br. et R.

This cactus generally grows singly amidst stones. The body is almost cylindrical, 30 to 35 mm high and 25 to 28 mm across. The crown is rounded, blunt, almost oblique, with a marked depression in the centre. The underground part of the stem is also cylindric, shaped like an upside-down egg, almost tuberous, terminating in a conical root. The body has 24 longitudinal ribs, perpendicularly or spirally arranged, coloured soft green or ashy grey, furrowed with shallow, distinctly marked, closely set lines. The tubercles are low, 3 to 4 mm across, with a shallow, narrow depression at the top. This is covered with white felt and bears about a dozen 1 to 2 mm-long, thin, white, practically pectinate spines arranged in two rows, six spines to each. The fairly large flowers, emerging on the side of the stem about one third of the way down, are about 32 mm across and coloured orange with a rich yellow base. The stamens are smooth and yellow, the anthers yellow or a paler shade, the style whitish-yellow, terminated by an 8 to 12 lobed cream-coloured stigma.

Lobivia famatimensis, introduced as a commercial species by C. Backeberg, has become well known for its bright flowers ranging from yellow to red with a wide variety of shades. It has many varieties and forms distributed over a wide range, where they occur as mountain cacti. In cultures they bear proliferous flowers in a wide range of colours at the beginning of the summer. They are a source of great pleasure to cactus growers, especially when cultivated in the open, without glass. In winter they require a cool, dry atmosphere. They are generally propagated from shoots which are grown on their own roots or grafted on Cereus stock.

Lobivia jajoiana Backbg.

Cactus growing singly or in groups. The stem is spherical, 5 to 7 cm across, becoming columnar in age. The crown is slightly depressed and covered with whitish wool and several spines. The colour is a glossy, bright green. The ribs, 12 to 14, run downward at a slant and are divided into tubercles whose arrangement creates the impression of a wavy line. The areoles, 3 mm across, have grey-white felt. The spines are pale and blackish-brown in youth, later grey. The radial spines, 8 to 10, are about 1 cm long. The central spines, 1 to 3, are stronger, dark, frequently red; the upper spine attains a length of 3 cm and is hooked. The flowers are 6.5 cm across, tomato red, with dark purple throat, thickened at the edge and glossy. The stamens are purple, the anthers yellow.

Habitat: Northern Argentina — Province of Salta, elevation 9000 ft.

This is a very popular species for its interesting flowers. Several different varieties are to be found in collections; var. *fleischeriana* is distinguished by long (up to 5 cm), hooked spines, var. *splendens* by broad petals, var. *nigrostoma* by yellow flowers.

This cactus is easily grown along with other *Lobivias*. It requires a clean, moist atmosphere and adequate light, but does not however tolerate exposure to the noon-day sun. In winter it needs light, a dry atmosphere and temperature of 6 to 8°C. It is easily propagated from shoots produced by adult plants or from the seed. Seedlings attain maturity within 3 to 4 years.

Lobivia wrightiana Backbg.

This cactus belongs to the group of Lobivias which have a large turnip-like root and small, ash-green body with thin, partly hooked spines. In age the plant may bear markedly long, thin spines often variously curved, which are characteristic of the species. *Lobivia wrightiana* has 15 to 17 spirally arranged ribs separated by faint, shallow grooves. The radial spines number about 10 and are barely 1 cm long. Not till later does the plant bear up to 7 cm long, antenna-like spines. The delicate flowers are a lovely lilac-pink. The fruit is reddish, and measures about 6 mm across.

It occurs in the Mantanaro River Valley in Central Peru.

Most Lobivias grow in soil that is not very rich but some are fresh green plants (*L. hertrichiana, L. binghamiana, L. allegraiana, L. incaica* and *L. planiceps*), that grow in territory with more rain and soil richer in humus. Their flowers are red and proliferous, appearing sometimes throughout the whole summer in Europe. This is a particularly welcome trait, especially in Lobivias, for all other species of this genus flower only in early summer and rarely again in autumn.

The genera *Lobivia, Mediolobivia* and *Rebutia* are typical mountain cacti (just as most species of the genus *Parodia*, etc.) which grow best when provided with ample sunlight and fresh air, without the heat of the greenhouse. In winter they require light and a cooler atmosphere to prevent growth and deformation. Such cacti do poorly indoors and in cities, in the same way as alpine plants.

Lophophora williamsii (Lem. ex SD.) Coult.

The body is soft, elastic, grey-green, broader than it is high, 5 to 8 cm across, branching in age. The underground extension of the body is a strong, turnip-like root, 10 to 15 cm long. The 5 to 15 ribs are shallow, divided in some forms into tubercles that bear tufts of matted hair forming a thick cover of yellow-white or grey-white wool on the crown. From this cover emerge large, pale violet flowers with darker central stripe that arises throughout the whole growing period. The fruit is a red, fleshy berry which is borne in the second year. The seed is small, black.

Habitat: Mexico and the United States. It grows on both banks of the lower reaches of the Rio Grande on the U.S.-Mexican border, but also elsewhere in Mexico; its best-known locality is the town of Laredo.

The genus *Lophophora* is one of the strangest, most interesting of all cacti. Native Indians knew of its narcotic effects long before the arrival of the white man. In the Mexico of old, where many cacti were worshipped as gods, the cult of the peyote was undoubtedly the most widespread. Supernatural powers were ascribed to this root; persons who eat it were able to see into the future and foretell future events. Missionaries forbade consumption of peyote, calling it the devil's root, for the ceremonies and superstitions were linked with the old Aztec religion.

Lophophora williamsii is one of the hardiest of the known cacti, growing where even the Pelargonia will not survive. It requires heavier, nourishing soil and adequate light, in winter a dry atmosphere, light and a temperature of 10°C.

Plate 38

Mamillaria applanata Eng.

As the name indicates (*applanata* — flattened) this is a plant of small height, a fairly rare trait in cacti of this genus for most Mamillarias, especially in European cultures, are club-shaped or tall cylindrical forms. Of the related species (*M. heyderi, M. hemisphaerica* and others) *M. applanata* is often the flattest, for with a diameter of more than 10 cm it attains a height of only 2.5 to 5 cm and in addition has a depressed crown covered with white wool. The areoles on the flattened, angular tubercles bear 15 to 20 radial spines, whitish, 5 to 12 mm long, and one stronger erect central spine coloured brown with a black tip. The flowers, appearing in May, are about 2 cm long and up to 3.5 cm broad, cream to pinkish on the inside. The fruit is red, more than 3 cm long and contains brownish-red seeds. *M. applanata* and related plants have also been named *M. texensis* as they grow predominantly in central and southern Texas.

Mamillaria applanata as well as *M. melanocentra* and other low or flat spherical Mamillarias are especially well suited for cultivation in window gardens for they are fairly hardy species that do not attain great dimensions and remain fine specimens even in age when other Mamillarias lose their attractive shape, and their stem bases turn brown and become covered with dead tubercles. Cactus growers should pay greater notice to older species (*M. applanata* was described as early as 1850) as some of their beautiful forms may soon become scarce.

Mamillaria bocasana Pos.

This is a small, spherical plant, making side shoots freely
as a rule. The individual stems of this green to blue-green
Mamillaria measure only about 4 to 5 cm and are completely covered with fine, grey-white spines almost
entirely concealing the soft and slightly conical tubercles.
The number of radial spines is truly great, 25 to 30.
Besides that, there are the yellow to reddish, needle-like
central spines, terminating in a thin hook, which measure
20 mm or more in length, the greyish, hair-like radial
spines being much shorter. Amidst these thick hairs the
flowers are not very conspicuous. They are about 15 mm
long, 10 mm broad, yellowish with a central reddish
stripe on the outer petals. As if to offset this, however,
M. bocasana flowers profusely and often even in modest
circumstances.

A great favourite is the variety *splendens* (*splendens* =
shining, glossy). Also known are plants that have a particularly dense coat of white spines, the lower spines
usually being yellow and hooked. All these cacti can be
recommended to the beginner for they can withstand even
mistakes in treatment, e.g. unsuitable location, just like
the hardiest of other Mamillaria species (*M. gracilis*,
M. pusilla, *M. wildii*, etc.).

Besides the cactus described here, Mamillarias include
a number of so-called soft as well as fairly hard species
that are also easy to grow. For example, *M. centricirrha*,
M. hidalgengensis, etc. which can both be grown in window
gardens along with other hardy cacti and succulents.

Mamillaria bombycina Quehl.

This lovely and well-known plant forms stems measuring about 6 cm across and up to 20 cm high. It often branches freely and in age the clumps then form huge groups. The pale green heads are covered with conical to cylindric nipples with thick white wool growing out of their axils. The many radial spines, 30 to 40, are 2 to 10 mm long and white. The central spines, usually 2 to 4, are about 10 mm long, the lower one attaining a length of 2 cm and terminating in a hook. The central spines are fairly weak but unlike the radial spines they are usually yellowish with brownish-red tips. The lovely flowers measure 1.5 cm both in length and in breadth; they are pale carmine with a darker centre. The whitish, club-shaped fruits contain small black seeds.

Mamillaria bombycina, the latin name indicating that the plant has silky, shining spines (*bombycina* = silky), originates, like most Mamillarias, in Mexico. It is one of the loveliest species of this genus, thanks to the contrast of its coloured spines.

Mamillaria bombycina was described prior to World War I when the first specimens were imported from Mexico by the firm De Laet of Belgium, and it soon won a reputation as one of the most beautiful plants of this genus. It is a fairly robust and hardy cactus which can be grown on its own roots. When grafted on sturdy stock *M. bombycina* soon forms a magnificent clump of robust stems. It must be handled with care, however, for the spines are prone to catch and are easily broken off, despite the fact that this species does not belong to the group with milky sap.

Plate 41

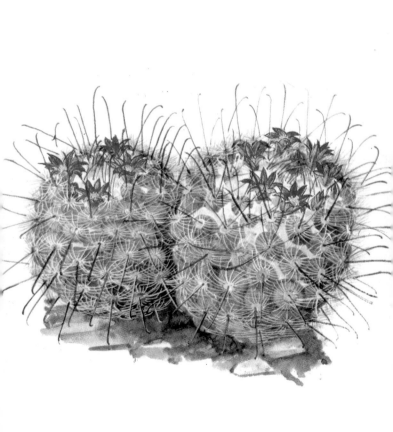

Mamillaria centricirrha Lem.

This cactus has a dark green, globose, later cylindrical body, 10 cm or more across and up to 30 cm high, branching freely from the base in age. The nipples are angular, 2 cm long, arranged in spiralled rows. The axils and areoles bear thick, whitish wool. The 4 to 5 radial spines are awl-shaped, about 2 cm long, straight or slightly curved; there is one central spine. All are a pale colour with dark tip. The flowers form a wreath at the top of the plant. They are about 2.5 cm across, pale pink with darker central stripe. They emerge from the end of April till June in several rows one after the other. The fruit is a club-shaped, fleshy carmine berry, the seed is small and pale brown.

Habitat: Mexico.

The specific name *centricirrha* means in the centre, central.

Mamillaria centricirrha is considered by some authorities to be synonymous with *Mamillaria magnimamma* which bears yellowish flowers. Craig lists 116 synonyms, more than half of them as varieties of *Mamillaria centricirrha*. Specimens grown in Europe for more than a hundred years are partly cross-bred and thus the individual varieties or forms cultivated in collections have mutual characters and their separation is difficult. The best known varieties are *bockii*, *divergens*, *recurva* and *krameri* described by K. Schumann. *M. centricirrha* is a common species with proliferous flowers which is recommended to beginners for its easy cultivation. Even fairly small plants flower every year if they have sufficient heat, light and moisture during the growing period. It is easily propagated from the seed, which has good powers of germination, even three to four year-old seedlings bearing flowers.

Mamillaria hahniana Werd.

A spherical, solitary specimen at first, this cactus later forms large clumps of heads up to 10 cm in diameter. The nipples are small, up to 5 mm long, spherical or triangular, narrowed at the tip with a blunt point and coloured green. The axils develop short white wool and tufts of white bristles up to 4 cm long. The areoles are small, elliptic, with short white felt which is later shed. The radial spines, some 20 to 30, are white, hair-like, flexible, 5 to 15 mm long and wavy. The single central spine is straight, acicular, up to 4 mm long, with a brown tip. The flowers emerge near the crown and form a wreath; they are funnel-shaped, 12 to 15 mm broad, wine-red with greenish-white throat. The fruit is club-shaped, pinkish-red, the seed 1 mm long and pale brown.

Habitat: Mexico — Guanajuato.

Mamillaria hahniana, also known as the ,,Old Lady", is one of the most beautiful species of Mamillaria; in youth it greatly resembles the "Old Man" Cactus — *Cephalocereus senilis*. Also cultivated in cultures are the varieties *giselana* and *werdermanniana*, differing from the type by the shorter hairs. The flowers emerge at the end of May in the form of a wreath, creating a bright contrast with the long, white hairs which completely cover the plant. Like all Mamillarias it is comparatively easy to grow, although in the dusty atmosphere of cities it has grey hairs and a droopy appearance. During the growing period it requires heat, moisture, sunlight and clean air, in winter light and a cooler, dry atmosphere. It is easily propagated from the seed.

Mamillaria sheldonii (Br. et R.) Böd.

The body is cylindrical, 10 to 25 cm high, 6 cm across, dark green with brownish-red tint in the sun. The cylindrical, fairly short tubercles are terminated by round or oval, slightly wavy areoles, bearing 10 to 15 radial spines, white, 6 to 9 mm long, and 1 to 3 central spines, generally only one, thicker, about 12 mm long, porrect, reddish-brown, hooked. The flowers arise on the upper part of the stem, are about 3 cm broad, pale pink with pale edge. The fruit is a red berry, the seed (1 mm) is black.

Habitat: Mexico, Sonora.

Small, hook-spined Mamillarias are continually growing in popularity and their numbers are numerous; many belong to the so-called basic species such as *Mamillaria bocasana*, *M. longicoma*, *M. bombycina*, which are recommended to beginners for their ease of cultivation. Most highly prized are the small species with thick, brightly-coloured hooked spines. Among the best known and most frequently cultivated, besides *M. sheldonii*, is *M. swinglei*. The two show a marked similarity. *M. blossfeldiana* has yellowish-brown spines, flowers measuring about 2 cm, pale pink with darker central stripe. *M. dioica* attains a height of 25 cm and bears flowers 1 to 2 cm broad, yellow-white with red central stripe. *M. fraileana* has a columnar growth attaining a height of about 15 cm, the flowers are pink with darker central stripe.

Mamillaria sheldonii does fairly well in heavier, clay, porous soil, requiring plenty of light and in the growing period also heat. It does not tolerate continual moisture. In winter it needs light and tolerates a cool, dry atmosphere. Seedlings are delicate in the first year; they need not be grafted.

Plate 44

Mamillaria zeilmanniana Böd.

The body is globose or ovoid, about 6 cm high and 4.5 cm across. The colour is a glossy dark green. The crown is slightly depressed and covered with young spines. The tubercles are dense, ovoid or short cylindrical, about 6 mm long and 3 to 4 mm thick. The areoles are covered with white felt which is soon shed. Radial spines, about 15 to 18, radiating, white, distinctly downy, very thin, erect or slightly bent, 1 cm long. The central spines, 4, are reddish-brown, 8 mm long — three are straight, the lowest is longer and hooked. Flowers appear near the crown in the form of a wreath, are purplish-red or violet, paler at the base, about 1.5 to 2 cm across. The filaments are purplish-red, the anthers yellow. The style is green at the base, purplish-red at the top with a four-lobed, yellow stigma. The fruit is a small, whitish-green berry, the seed, 1 mm large, is black.

Habitat: Mexico — Guanajuato near San Miguel Allende.

The specific name *zeilmanniana* is after H. Zeilmann, member of the German Cactus Society.

It was discovered in 1931 by E. Georgi of Saltilla growing in stony ground. It belongs to the group of fleshy, hook-spined species such as *M. trichacantha*, *M. pubispina*, *M. hirsuta*, *M. longicoma*, *M. kunzeana* and *M. bocasana*, all bearing white flowers. The cultivation of fleshy Mamillarias is not difficult. They do not tolerate continual watering. In the growing period *M. zeilmanniana* requires a sunny and warm site and adequate water — care must be taken to prevent the roots rotting. In winter it needs a dry atmosphere, light and a temperature of up to 10°C. The soil should be porous with crushed brick. It is propagated well from the seed.

Mediolobivia aureiflora Backbg.

In youth the body is simple, globose, about 5 cm across, later it sends out side shoots freely and forms clumps of stems. The colour is dull green, tinged with brown in the sun. The crown is slightly depressed and covered with spines. The tubercles are arranged in 15 to 17 spiralled rows, 3 to 4 mm high. The areoles are 1 to 2 mm long, covered with thin, white wool and bearing 13 to 20 spines, about 6 mm long, 3 or 4 of them more central and measuring 1 cm in length or over. The flowers are 4 to 4.5 cm long, with broad limb, 4 cm across, orange-yellow with whitish throat. The stamens are a creamy colour, arranged in two circles, the anthers are yellow. The style and stigma are creamy. The ovary is glossy, pale olive red, about 5 mm across.

Habitat: Northern Argentina, Province of Salta, where it grows on the rocky hills.

The specific name *aureiflora* means golden-flowered.

This is a popular species, very variable in colour as well as in the length of the spines and the flowers. Specialized collections contain several interesting varieties, namely:
Mediolobivia aureiflora var. *albiseta*
    ,,   ,,   var. *boedeckeriana*
    ,,   ,,   var. *rubelliflora*
    ,,   ,,   var. *sarothroides*
    ,,   ,,   var. *duursmaniana*
This species grows very well from the seed or grafted on higher stock of *Piptanthocereus peruvianus*, *P. dayami*, and the like, on which it flowers sooner and more profusely. The plant requires plenty of light and fresh air, in winter light and a temperature of up to 8°C.

Mediolobivia ritteri (Wessn.) Krainz

This cactus forms clumps of small, round or oval, dark green bodies with reddish-purple tinge. The ribs, about 15, are divided by grooves into low tubercles. The areoles are elliptic, covered with a yellowish felt. The spines, 8 to 10, are radiating, thin, pale brown, 0.8 to 1 cm long. The flowers are broad funnel-shaped, about 4.5 cm across, glossy, vermilion with purplish-red throat. The stamens are carmine, the style and stigma greenish-yellow. The fruit is 0.5 cm across, covered with wool and bristles. The seed is small, dull black.

Habitat: Bolivia, elevation 10,200 ft.

The specific name is in honour of the collector F. Ritter. The genus *Mediolobivia* marks the transition between the genus *Lobivia* and the evolutionarily more advanced genera *Aylostera* and *Rebutia*.

Mediolobivia ritteri is a well known and popular species belonging to the same group as *M. euanthema*. This has short, white, bristly spines. The flower tube is meaty-red, the flowers measure 3.5 cm across, the inside is coloured red and orange, the filaments dark carmine. It grows on the border of Bolivia and Argentina like the variety *oculata*, which differs from the type by its bright green flower tube and broader orange petals. A fairly widespread species is *M. eucaliptana*, of Bolivia, which is clustered and has pale, delicate, slightly curved spines. Its proliferous flowers are a brick red. *Mediolobivia costata* grows singly, later forming clumps, the dark green body being divided into 8 to 9 ribs.

In the growing period M. ritteri requires light, heat and adequate water, in winter a light, dry atmosphere with temperature of up to 10°C and adequate fresh air.

Neochilenia jussieuii (Monv.) Backbg.

The body is globose, later cylindrical, about 8 to 10 cm across, brownish-green, with dark purple tinge. The ribs, 13 to 16, are divided by cross grooves, the areoles are large with yellow felt. The radial spines number 7 to 14, the central, 1 to 2, are longer, up to 2.5 cm in length and slightly curved. All are pale at first, later brown with dark tip. The flowers are funnel-shaped, measuring up to 4 cm, glossy, pale orange with darker stripe. The stamens greenish, the 6 lobed stigma red.

Habitat: Chile.

The specific name is in honour of Prof. A. L. Jussieu of Paris.

This is without a doubt one of the handsomest flower-bearing cacti of all the Chilean species. Despite this, it is rarely found in collections for it is prey to the "brown fungus", a disease to which all Chilean cacti are prone and which, even after eradication, leaves deep ugly scars. *N. jussieuii* is often mistaken for other species of this genus. Related species include *Neochilenia fobeana,* which has a thick cover of hard spines and orange-red flowers. *N. occulta* is brown with irregularly spaced spines, 1 to 4 cm long, and yellow flower with reddish stripe. *Neochilenia fusca* is dark green with 13 radial spines, 1 to 2 central spines 3 cm long, and yellow flowers.

In cultures all Chilean species require sufficient fresh air and heat, in winter adequate light and a dry, fairly cool atmosphere. This species is usually propagated from the seed; small seedlings are grafted on hybrid *Echinopsis* or on short stock of *Eriocereus jusbertii.*

Notocactus concinnus (Monv.) Berg.

A small, flat, globe-shaped body, 6 cm high and up to 10 cm across, glossy, fresh green with 16 to 20 low, blunt tuberculate ribs. The areoles are small with short, white felt which is later shed. Radial spines, 10 to 12, are thin, bristly, 5 to 7 mm long, pale yellow. The four central spines, set crosswise, are yellow and brown at the base; the lower spine is strongest and up to 2 cm long, the other 3 are shorter, about 1.5 cm long. The flowers emerge on the crown, often several at a time. They measure about 7 cm, are funnel-shaped, yellow inside, glossy. The filaments are yellow, carmine at the base, the anthers are yellow. The style is carmine at the base, yellow at the top, with 10-lobed, carmine stigma. The fruit is dry, hairy, covered with brown bristly spines. The seed measures 1 mm and is grey.

Habitat: Southern Brazil, Uruguay.

The specific name *concinnus* means gentle.

Notocactus concinnus was discovered by Sellow in Uruguay and imported to Paris in 1838. One year later it was described by Monville as *Echinocactus concinnus*. In their native land Notocacti are often found growing together with Gymnocalycia in grass in fairly damp sites. They do well in a partially shaded, light locality, and require heavier, rich, porous soil. The growing period begins in early spring, buds usually beginning to form on the crown in April. Application of water is commenced after the buds are developed. In the heat of the summer months water is applied lightly. Mid-August marks the beginning of the new growing period which lasts till the end of September. In winter the plant requires light and a drier atmosphere with temperature of about 10°C. It is propagated easily from the seed which has good powers of germination. Seedlings usually bear flowers in the third year.

Obregonia denegrii Frič

The body is about 10 cm across and 6 cm high, the base
terminating in a strong, turnip-like root. The stem is dark
green; imported plants or those grown in bright sun are
greyish-green with a pinkish tinge. The triangular tubercles are spirally arranged — they are thick, 2 to 2.5 cm
across at the base and 1.5 cm long, with areoles at the tip
bearing 2 to 4 spines. These are pale yellow, thin, about
1.5 cm long with darker tip. The flowers arise from the
youngest areoles, are whitish or cream-coloured, about
2 cm across. The flower tube and ovary are almost naked.
After the flower has dried the ovary recedes into the plant
and when ripe a soft white berry, like that of Ariocarpus
or Melocactus, appears in the thick white wool.

Habitat: The calciferous desert in Lanos del Joumave
in the state of Taumalipas, Mexico.

The generic name *Obregonia* is after the Mexican
president Alvaro Obregon.

The specific name *denegrii* is in honour of the Mexican
Minister of Agriculture Denegri.

Obregonia denegrii is a monotypic genus, a transition
between *Ariocarpus, Strombocactus* and *Leuchtenbergia*. It
closely resembles the artichoke. It was discovered by
A. V. Frič in 1923.

Somewhat more difficult to grow, it is recommended to
graft this plant on hybrid *Echinopsis* on which it does very
well, bearing flowers within three years. Great favourites
are imported specimens that should be planted in porous,
clay soil with drainage. Imported plants should be watered with care as they do not tolerate excessive watering and
direct sunlight.

Plate 50

Opuntia microdasys   (Lehm.) Pfeiff.

A shrub-like cactus 60 cm to 1 m high, with flat, oval joints about 10 cm wide and 15 cm long, covered with down and coloured emerald green. The areoles are oval, 1 to 2 mm across, with yellowish, later brownish, felt with a vast number of golden-yellow glochids, arranged almost regularly into squares. The flowers, measuring about 4.5 cm, are golden-yellow inside, the filaments and anthers yellow, the style whitish. The fruit is a spherical red berry about 4 cm across. The seed is large, reddish-grey.

Habitat: Mexico — Durango, Coahuila, Chihuahua.

The specific name *microdasys* means with short down.

No collection of the early cactus growers was complete without some Opuntia, even though they later proved unsuitable for small collections by virtue of their size. There are, however, several species that form a bright spot in any collection. Among the prettiest is *Opuntia microdasys*, known as the "Golden Opuntia" whose greatest ornament are the yellow, white, or brownish-red glochids arranged in regular formation. Several varieties and forms are to be found in collections, the best known being *Opuntia microdasys* var. *albispina* with white tufts of glochids. This variety also includes the form *minima* with small joints, well suited for very small collections.

Opuntia microdasys is cultivated in rich, heavier soil. During the growing period it requires adequate moisture, sun and ventilation, in winter light, a dry atmosphere and temperature of 5° to 8°C. It is generally propagated from cuttings. The cuttings, having dried in the sun, are planted after about ten days in adequate pots filled with soil where they soon send out roots. The plant is only propagated from the seed by specialized cactus growers.

Oreocereus neocelsianus (Berg. et Ricc.) Backbg.

The stem is columnar, erect, attaining a height of 1 m and branching at a later age. The shoots are 8 to 12 cm thick, glossy green, later dark, with 10 to 17 ribs, 8 mm in height and divided by deep grooves. The areoles are oval, measuring 10 to 18 mm, with thick, yellow wool which later disappears. The areoles bear long (5 cm or more), white, wavy hairs which later turn grey. The nine radial spines are 2 cm long, radiating, the 1 − 4 central spines are up to 8 cm long. All spines are pale yellow, orange or red. The flowers, arising near the crown, are narrow, up to 10 cm long, strawberry red to pale brown. The filaments are greenish to brown, the anthers red to purplish-red. The pistil is brownish and is taller than the stamens. The ovary is spherical, covered with bristles and wool.

Habitat: Southern Bolivia to northern Argentina.

The authors describe several interesting varieties which are found today only in old collections.

Oreocereus neocelsianus was first brought from Bolivia by Bridges and described by him in 1850 as *Pilocereus celsianus*. In its habitat it forms clusters and stands of columnar bodies covered with long hairs, from which emerge strong, acicular, whitish to yellowish or red spines.

Oreocereus is not difficult to grow. It requires chiefly fresh air and sun, in summer heat and moisture; in winter light and a dry, cool atmosphere. It is grafted on strong stock or grown on its own roots in rich soil. It is generally propagated from the seed.

Plate 52

Parodia chrysacanthion (K. Sch.) Backbg.

The body is flattened, spherical, 8 to 10 cm across, slightly columnar in age, bright green, the crown covered with white, flaky wool. The entire plant is densely covered with straight, golden-yellow to honey-brown spines up to 4 cm long. The flowers emerge near the crown, are about 2 cm long and golden-yellow. They appear in early spring and arise continually for several months.

Habitat: Argentina — Province of Jujuy.

The specific name *chrysacanthion* means golden species.

The first Parodia was discovered by Schickendantz in 1886 in the mountains of Tucuman Province near Catamarca. It was named *Echinocactus microspermus* by Dr. Weber for its microscopically small brown seeds. Six years later, in 1892, O. Kunze discovered another straight-spined plant in northern Argentina, quite different from *E. microspermus*, which Prof. Schumann named *Echinocactus chrysacanthion* for its golden spines in 1898. In 1926 Dr. C. Spegazzini introduced the generic name *Parodia* for these species, named after the Argentine botanist Parodi. *Parodia chrysacanthion* disappeared from collections for a number of years, only to return again after a time as an old, well-known species forgotten in the tide of novelties which flooded the market. Today more than 100 species are known.

Cultivation is not difficult. It is grown on its own roots in rich, porous soil with adequate light, heat and water. In winter it requires cold, light and adequate ventilation. It is propagated well from the seed.

Parodia mutabilis   Backbg.

The body is spherical or slightly columnar, 8 cm across
and up to 10 cm high, blue-green, the crown slightly
woolly. The spirally arranged ribs are divided into low
tubercles with small, white felted areoles. The radial
spines, about 50, are thin, pure white, radiating, the
4 central spines, arranged in the form of a cross, are 1 to
1.5 cm long, white, orange to brown; one is hooked. The
flowers are golden-yellow, more than 3 cm across, with
white or red throat. The fruit is small and round, the
seeds fine and brown.

Habitat: Argentina — Salta, elevation 8400 ft.

The specific name *mutabilis* means changeable.

This species was found and described by Frič's pupil
C. Backeberg, globe-trotter and collector of cacti as well as
author of the most extensive monograph on the subject.
The habitat of *Parodia mutabilis* is the Province of Salta
with its warm climate, located in the foothills of the
Andes. It is here that most of the species and varieties
described by Backeberg are to be found, e.g. *Parodia
aureicentra*, *P. aureispina*, *P. erythrantha*, *P. scopaoides*,
P. setifera, *P. rubricentra* and also three, according to the
author, different varieties of *Parodia mutabilis*, namely
P. mutabilis var. *carneospina*, var. *elegans* and var. *ferru-
ginea*.

In Europe varieties lose their characteristic features,
especially in later generations, and in collections varieties
are often cross-pollinated. *Parodia mutabilis* is easy to
cultivate. In the growing period it requires sufficient light
(but does not tolerate direct sunlight), moisture and rich,
porous soil. In winter light and a dry atmosphere with
temperature of 5° to 8°C. It is propagated from the seed.

Parodia nivosa Frič ex. Backbg.

The body is spherical to slightly columnar, 8 cm across
and up to 15 cm high, pale green with olive tinge. The
ribs are composed of spirally arranged conical tubercles.
The areoles are white-felted. The radial spines, about 18,
are sometimes more than 1 cm long, the central spines, 4,
arranged crosswise, are stronger and more than 2 cm long.
All are glassy white, the central spines sometimes brownish. The flowers arise on the crown, often several at a
time, are blood-red, 3 to 5 cm across. The stamens and
8 lobed stigma are yellowish. The ovary is small, round,
covered with white hairs and bristles. The seed is small,
black-brown.

Habitat: Northern Argentina — Province of Salta.

Parodia nivosa grows in the north-western tip of Argentina in a region that is rich in cacti and is also one of
Argentina's most attractive holiday areas. A. V. Frič was
carried away by the beauty of the plant when he discovered it. It belongs to the group of miniature alpine
species of straight-spined Parodias, the same as *Parodia
faustiana*, *P. crucinigricentra* and *P. crucialbicentra*. Unlike
Parodia nivosa, *P. crucinigricentra* and *P. crucialbicentra*,
which A. V. Frič discovered on his last trip in 1928 to
1929, bear yellow flowers and are true rarities. *Parodia
nivosa* requires much light, fresh air and adequate water in
the growing period. It does well on its own roots in good,
nourishing soil. The seedlings may also be grown grafted
on hybrid *Echinopsis*. In winter the plant requires light,
water (only in the case of a graft), and temperature of 7° to
10°C. It is propagated only from the seed.

Parodia sanguiniflora Frič ex. Backbg.

The body is spherical, becoming columnar in age, fresh green, 5 to 8 cm across, 10 cm or more high. The ribs comprise spirally arranged, conical tubercles. The white-felted areoles bear 15 thin white radial spines, 6 to 8 mm long. The four central spines are brown, arranged in the form of a cross. The lowest is hooked and up to 2 cm long. The flowers arise near the crown, are blood-red, about 4 cm across. The filaments are carmine at the top and orange to pale yellow at the base; the anthers are yellow. The style is white with 11 lobed stigma, taller than the stamens. The ovary is round, dry, about 6 mm across; the seed is very small and brown.

Habitat: Argentina — Province of Salta.

The specific name *sanguiniflora* means bearing red flowers.

Parodia sanguiniflora is one of the plants discovered by A. V. Frič in the mountains of Salta already in 1928 and introduced by him to Europe under the name of *Microspermia sanguiniflora*. This, however, did not enter into common usage. Dr. Spegazzini transferred these cacti to the genus *Parodia*. Prior to World War I there were only three known species of *Parodia* and it was not till Frič discovered new localities of their occurrence that a wave of new species appeared on the market. Today *Parodia* species rank among the more popular cacti. Their habitat is the mountains of north-western Argentina and neighbouring Bolivia and broad regions of Paraguay as well as south and west Brazil. The number of species totals about 100 and new ones are continually being discovered.

Most Parodias grow well on their own roots. During the growing period, however, they require adequate water, sun and heat. In winter they should be placed in a light, ventilated and fairly cool spot with temperature ranging from 5° to 10°C. It is generally propagated from the seed which has good powers of germination, but the seedlings are very small.

Pilosocereus palmeri (Rose) Byl. et Rowl.

The plant is erect, either shrub form or arborescent, 2 to
6 m high, with about 20 branches. The individual stems
are about 8 cm across, dark or pale green. The ribs, 7 to 9,
are broad and blunt. The radial spines, from 8 to 12, are
weak, 2 to 3 cm long, the single central spine is about 3 cm
long. All spines are brown or grey. The flowers are pink,
bell-shaped, about 6 cm across. They open in the evening
and remain open till dawn; they have an unpleasant odour.
The fruit is globose, about 6 cm in diameter, the seed is
black and glossy.

Habitat: Mexico — Tamaulipas.

C. Backeberg describes also *P. palmeri* var. *victoriensis*,
differing only slightly from the type. It has white petals
with a violet tinge. It grows in the State of Victoria, hence
its specific name. Some authorities consider this variety
a synonym.

Pilosocerei are among the most widespread columnar
cacti and always belonged to the elite of European collections, though most species never attained the flower bearing stage under continental conditions. *P. palmeri* in
cultivation bears flowers by the time it has attained a
height of 1 m; these arise from the thick wool on the
crown. Cultivation of this plant is not difficult. It attains
a considerable height, however, so that it can be grown
only in greenhouses where it has ample space. During the
growing period it requires adequate application of water.
In winter it is somewhat intolerant of cold. A rich soil is
required. It is propagated from the seed.

Plate 57

Phyllocactus hybridus

The term Phyllocactus relates to hybrids resulting from the crossing of original botanical species or from their crossing with large-flowered Cerei. The original species come from Mexico and Honduras, Guatemala and Brazil, where they grow as epiphytes in the forks of trees or in the humus in chinks in rocks. The form is that of a shrub, the leaf-like, expanded shoots generally hanging downward and terminating at the end in aerial roots which serve for climbing and supplying nourishment.

The generic name *Phyllocactus* is of old Greek origin meaning leafy cactus.

Window boxes generally contain some hybrid of this genus, along with other plants, where it flowers from spring to summer in widely varied colours — red, pink, creamy or yellow as well as in multi-colour combinations. The flowers are simple and double, up to 20 cm in diameter. These beautiful hybrids are easy to grow. They show signs of life in early spring, beginning to bud sometimes even in February. They should be grown in a spot with ample light, slight watering and at room temperature until the flowers emerge; these last from late April till July. The ensuing rest period of several weeks is followed by the chief growing period which lasts till September when the new shoots attain full growth. In winter they should be kept in a cool spot with slight watering until February. Phyllocacti may be grown in any spot without direct sunlight, best of all between windows facing east, on a glassed verandah, or in summer in a shaded and sheltered spot in the garden. They are usually transplanted after the flowers have shrivelled into rich, coarse-grained, porous soil. They are generally propagated from the leaf-like, approximately 20 cm long shoots, which after the cut surface has dried, are planted in light sandy soil.

Pseudolobivia aurea (Br.et R.) Backbg.

This cactus does not attain large dimensions. The type is spherical, about 10 cm across with perpendicular ribs and dull green skin. The erect, hard, brown spines are about 10 to 30 mm long so that the plant resembles the common small Echinopsis. When in flower, however, it attracts notice from afar with its golden-yellow blooms measuring more than 10 cm in length and 8 cm across. These have caused this cactus to be dubbed the "Star of Cordoba" by the natives in the region of Cordoba, Argentina, which is its habitat.

Pseudolobivia aurea has many related forms differing from the type in the shape of the petals (e.g. in *var. elegans* they are narrower and more pointed, whereas in var. *grandiflora* they are broad), in the shape of the body, and in the colour and density of the spines. All, however, bear flowers of the same bright yellow so that the plant's name (*aurea* — golden) was truly well chosen. In recent years further related plants have been discovered thus confirming the fact that this is a single species with numerous variations and forms growing in various localities.

These pretty cacti are easy to grow and all are rewarding flower bearers so that it may be hoped that the "Star of Cordoba" will survive in collections even after it has become extinct in its natural habitat as a result of spreading cultivation.

It is worth noting that the genus *Pseudolobivia* was formed for the South American cacti considered by Backeberg as a transition between the thermophilic and columnar plants of the genus *Echinopsis*, which bear white, nocturnal flowers with long tubes, and the small mountain Lobivias, which bloom in the daytime, their flowers small and brightly coloured with shorter tubes. Their size and proliferous flowers make Pseudolobivias suitable cacti even for the smallest of collections.

Pseudolobivia kermesina Krainz.

This plant has a fresh green, semi-spherical to spherical stem, which when cultivated in rich soil attains a diameter of 15 cm or more. The ribs, 15 to 23 (in age even more), are low but up to 15 mm wide, expanded at the areoles and divided by marked grooves so that they may be described as tuberculate. The numerous thin spines (11 to 16 radial, and 4 to 6 central) are about 12 mm long (the central up to 25 mm long), yellow-rusty, with brown tips, later becoming grey. The plant's chief ornaments are the flowers which attain a length of 18 to 20 cm and width of 9 cm. They are green on the outside, the tube covered with greenish scales and grey wool. The petals, up to 6 cm long and 2 cm wide, are a bright carmine-red; the stamens are also carmine-red, the style pink and the stigma yellow. This beautiful plant was discovered by the German-born Argentine collector Vatter, who records Argentina as the habitat without any more precise details.

Pseudolobivia kermesina, so named for its bright carmine-red flowers (kermesina — carmine-red) is easily grown from the seed in Europe and is comparatively uniform even though there are certain racial deviations which re... hereditary according to the plant's locality in the wild. This cactus grows well on its own roots and tolerates even very rich soil, in which the seedlings grow to become strong specimens capable of bearing several flowers at a time.

In recent years several red-flowered Pseudolobivias have been discovered. In 1942, when *P. kermesina* was discovered, cactus growers knew mostly only white-flowered Pseudolobivias, except for *P. aurea*, which was generally classed with Echinopsis. The first *Pseudolobivia* bearing carmine-red flowers created a true sensation and even today is regarded as one of the loveliest cacti in European collections.

Rebutia marsoneri Werd.

The body is flattened, spherical, rarely sending out shoots. In age, it attains a height of 6 cm and diameter of 8 cm. The crown is depressed and only slightly spiny. The colour is pale green, later becoming grey at the base. The ribs are divided into small, often spirally arranged tubercles that are only 2 mm high and set 25 to 40 mm apart. The spines, 20 to 35, are difficult to separate into radial and central; they are 20 mm long and bright yellow with brown tip. Some forms have spines ranging from glassy white to rich shades of yellow. The flowers generally appear at the base of the stem. The buds are naked, coloured an intense red. The flowers are golden-yellow, up to 4 cm across. The filaments and anthers are pale yellow, the stigma white. The seed is small, black with white testa.

Habitat: Northern Argentina, Province of Jujuy.

The plant was discovered in 1935 by H. Blossfeld and O. Marsoner, whose name the species carries. The discovery of this golden-flowered *Rebutia* created a sensation among cactus growers for the hitherto known Rebutias, had always borne flowers in various shades of red. Although further yellow-flowered specimens of *Rebutia marsoneri* were discovered after a time by E. Vatter, most are without name, being assigned only a number. *R. marsoneri* grows best on its own roots or grafted on *Piptanthocereus peruvianus* on which it soon bears flowers. During the growing period it requires sunlight, air and adequate water, in winter light and a dry atmosphere and temperature of 7° to 10°C. It is propagated from the seed.

Rebutia senilis Backbg.

The body is up to 8 cm high, 6 to 7 cm wide, branching freely at the base. The colour is rich green, the base greyish. The spines are delicate, up to 3 cm long, pure white, soft, straight, some erect. Their number varies from 20 to 25. The flower is carmine-red, 3.5 cm broad. The fruit is pear-shaped, 4 to 6 mm across, and yellow-orange. The seed is small, black, the testa white.

Habitat: Northern Argentina, Province of Salta.

The specific name *senilis* means old.

Around 1930, when the cactus fever in Europe was at its height, South America was host to many cactus collectors. No wonder that the newly discovered, easily and proliferously flowering Rebutias were the vogue of the day. Of them all *Rebutia senilis* was perhaps the most outstanding for its abundance of beautiful flowers and snow-white spines. Rebutias, including *Rebutia senilis*, easily produce ample numbers of seeds with great powers of germination without the necessity of pollination. In its habitat *Rebutia senilis* forms clumps, growing amidst various grasses and low shrubs. In a limited range one will find numerous varieties and forms, many of which are cultivated by specialists. These include:

R. senilis var. *lilacino-rosea* Backbg. — pale lilac-rose flowers

R. senilis var. *breviseta* Backbg. — shorter spines, often interlaced

R. senilis var. *kesselringiana* Bewg. — pure yellow flowers

R. senilis var. *iseliniana* Krainz. — orange flowers, considered the handsomest variety of the whole species.

R. senilis is very easy to cultivate, best of all from the seed or from shoots grafted on Piptanthocerei.

Strombocactus disciformis (DC.) Br. et R.

The body is flattened, globose, 3 to 8 cm high, reaching 20 cm in age, and 3 to 9 cm across. The colour is blue-green with greyish tinge, the base covered with brown corky spots in age. The crown is slightly depressed and felted. The ribs are divided into rhomboid tubercles, 1 to 1.8 cm high. The spines, 4 to 5, are pale, 1.2 to 2 cm long, with dark tip, they become calcified in age and fall at the stem base. The flowers arise on the crown, measure about 3.5 cm in length and breadth, are pale yellow with several purple spots at the tip and in the throat. The filaments are white or reddish, the anthers yellow. The 8 to 10 lobed stigma is white or yellowish. The fruit, 7 mm across, splits down its length. The seed is very small — 0.3 mm.

Habitat: Mexico — Hidalgo.

The specific name *disciformis* means circular.

The first specimen was brought from Mexico by Coulter in 1829 and later by Ehrenberg in 1836. It is a very interesting and rare plant. The body, composed of hard, spirally arranged rhomboid tubercles, terminates in a strong turnip-like root. The cream coloured flowers emerge early in spring and remain open for several days. After the transfer of the other Strombocacti to *Turbini-carpus*, *Strombocactus disciformis* remains the only representative of the genus. It differs from Turbinicarpus by its body structure, flowers and size of the seeds, which are difficult to distinguish with the naked eye. It is cultivated chiefly as seedlings grafted on hybrid Echinopsis or on short stock of *Eriocereus jusbertii*, on which it soon flowers. During the growing period it requires heat, sun and adequate water, in winter light and a temperature of about 10°C with application of water only to grafted plants so that the stock does not dry up. It is generally propagated from the seed. Cultivation requires great patience.

Plate 63

Thelocactus bicolor (Gal.) Br. et R.

This cactus has a comparatively small, ovoid to cylindrical, pale green body, 10 to 15 cm high, 6 to 8 cm across, with 8 prominent ribs divided by deep grooves into tubercles with large, white-felted areoles. The areoles bear 9 to 18 yellowish, 2 to 3 cm long radial spines. The four central spines are longer, up to 5 cm, and red at the base. The flowers are large, about 6 cm in diameter, glossy, purplish-pink.

Habitat: Mexico and the United States — Texas.

The specific name *bicolor* means two-coloured.

Thelocactus bicolor is the most popular species of the whole genus. It is distinguished by beautiful coloured spines and large purplish-pink flowers which open in sunlight. The species has been known to collectors for more than 120 years. Thousands of specimens were imported to Europe in the days of the cactus craze, not only the type species but numerous varieties and local forms as well, all distinguished by brightly coloured spines. The most widespread is the variety *tricolor* which has yellow, red and white spines.

It is fairly easy to cultivate, the plants growing equally well from the seed or as imports from Mexico or Texas. They prefer abundant sunlight, during the growing period heat and careful application of water. In winter the plant will withstand a cool (5° to 8°C), dry atmosphere. It requires heavier, porous soil. It is propagated well from the seed which soon germinates; seedlings flower within four years. They need not be grafted.

Trichocereus candicans (Gill.) Br. et R.

The stem is globose in youth, later becoming columnar, 12 to 24 cm across and reaching a height of 75 cm. It branches freely from the base. The stem is pale green and glossy. The ribs, 9 to 12, are broad and blunt with large white-felted areoles. The radial spines, 10 to 12, are honey-yellow, 4 cm long; the central spines, 1 to 4, are erect and up to 10 cm long. The flowers are white, funnel-shaped, and up to 20 cm long. The large fruit is elliptic in shape.

Habitat: Argentina — Mendoza.

The specific name *candicans* means glossy white.

Also cultivated in collections is *Trichocereus candicans* var. *gladiatus*, differing from the type species by the lower and broader body, up to 24 cm across, and the strong longer (about 10 cm), yellow spines coloured red at the base. Var. *tenuispina* makes shoots freely but is little cultivated and then generally as stock. The whole genus *Trichocereus* belongs to the large group of columnar Cereus-type cacti distinguished by beautiful, usually long spines which are more ornamental than the flowers because they generally appear on older plants. The flowers are nocturnal. These cacti are particularly well suited for owners of greenhouses as they attain large dimensions. They are not difficult to grow and are well suited as stock for grafting and especially for beginners and youngsters. The soil should be rich and heavier. During the growing period they require adequate water, heat and partial shade, in winter light and a fairly warm atmosphere — temperature about 10°C. *T. candicans* propagates well from the seed, which has good powers of germination, or from shoots.

Turbinicarpus lophophoroides

(Werd.) Buxb. et Backbg.

The body is globose in youth, about 4 to 5 cm across, later becoming columnar and reaching a height of 6 to 8 cm. The root is turnip-like and the crown covered with thick, white felt. The colour is dull, grey-green. The ribs are divided into flat, 4 to 6 cornered tubercles, white at the top, generally with 3 to 4 pale, short spines and a single, 1 cm long central spine. The flowers are 3.5 cm in diameter, silky, glossy, and white with pink tinge. The stamens are yellow; the style and 4 lobed stigma white. The fruit is small and spherical with several, black seeds, 1 mm in size.

Habitat: Mexico — San Luis Potosi.

The plant was discovered by Sauer in 1934 in Mexico in the state of San Luis Potosi, where it grows at an elevation of 3600 ft. It is a rewarding species which flowers continually from early spring throughout the whole growing period bearing comparatively large, glossy, pink blossoms. All members of the genus *Turbinicarpus* are rare gems of Mexico's flora and the pride of every collector. The species *T. lophophoroides* is not particularly difficult to grow provided the plant is grafted on hybrid *Echinopsis* or on short stock of *Eriocereus jusbertii*. It requires adequate sunlight and water during the growth period, in winter light, heat and only slight watering so that the stock does not become too dry. It is generally propagated from the seed, the seedlings being grafted shortly after germination.

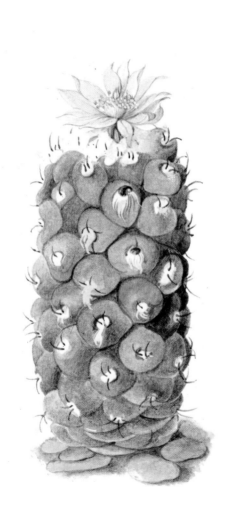

Zygocactus truncatus (Haw.) K. Sch.

Epiphyllum truncatum (Haw.)

The original botanical species of *Zygocactus truncatus* is an epiphyte growing on trees or damp rocks. It forms a short, woody, richly branched stem with broad, leaf-like joints. The flowers are zygomorphic, 6 to 8 cm long and pinkish-purple.

Habitat: Brazil — the foothills of Rio de Janeiro.

The specific name *truncatus* means truncate, lopped off.

It has been cultivated on window-sills along with Phyllocacti, Clivia and Echinopsis for more than a hundred years. By suitable hybridization and cultivation this species has enriched the assortment of plants flowering in winter. Original, so-called "pure" species have become of slight importance and are grown only in collections of botanical gardens.

Best suited for indoor, household cultivation are plants growing on their own roots, i.e. cultivated from joints planted directly in pots filled with sandy, nourishing soil. Plants grafted on stems of *Pereskia*, as they are usually sold in stores, are less suited for cultivation in dry apartments for the hygrophilous Pereskias lose their roots and cast off the joints and the cactus grower rarely succeeds in attaining a flower-bearing specimen. After the flowers have dried, they should be given a period of rest by placing them in a cooler spot and giving water sparingly. As soon as new joints begin to appear the plants are returned to a warmer and damper spot without direct sunlight. Around August when the new joints have attained full growth, the plant is given less water and placed in the spot where it is to flower. After the buds emerge the plant should not be moved, the temperature is increased and water is supplied lightly. The plants are transplanted into rich and porous soil after the flowers have died.

Aloe concinna Bak.

The lanceolate leaves arranged in a rosette are 10 to 15 cm long, 2 to 2.5 cm thick, their outer surface convex, pale green, covered with white elongate spots. The tips of the leaves are slightly curved downward, their edges toothed. The leaves dry from the stem base upward and fall, leaving a short, fairly small stem which makes shoots in age. The flowers emerge in early spring and several times more during the summer in the form of a simple or compound raceme, 10 to 25 cm long. The flowers, on short stalks, are 25 mm long and coloured orange with a green edge.

Habitat: Zanzibar.

The specific name *concinna* means gentle, lovely.

Aloe concinna is a comparatively little known species, distinguished by its decorative, white-spotted leaves. The plant is comparatively small when one considers that many species of *Aloe* are the size of trees, attaining a height of 2 to 4 metres. It tolerates the dust and smoke of cities fairly well.

Aloe concinna is successfully grown on window-sills between windows together with other ornamentals. During the growing period from April to May it requires adequate moisture, occasional application of liquid fertilizer, and rich, heavier soil. It is usually transplanted after 2 to 3 years and is propagated in spring or summer generally from the shoots growing from the base of the stem. These are put in pots filled with sandy soil where they soon take root. In winter water is applied sparingly, only so that the plant does not become too dry, and the temperature is maintained at 10° to 15° C.

Aloe variegata L.

Aloe variegata forms thick rosettes up to 30 cm high with ascending leaves, spirally arranged in three rows. The leaves are triangular, indented on the inner side, and coloured grey-green with whitish spots. They measure 12 cm or more in length and up to 3.5 cm in width. The edges are bordered with fine, white, gristly teeth. The flower raceme comprises 20 to 30 meaty-red to scarlet-purple, green-edged flowers. Larger plants flower every year in spring and early summer 3 to 6 times.

Habitat: South Africa — Cape Province.

The specific name *variegata* means variegated.

Aloe variegata, commonly known as the "Falcon Feather" or "Tiger Aloe" is perhaps the most widely fancied succulent of all. It has been cultivated for many decades in window gardens growing in the company of Echinopses, Phyllocacti, nutmeg, and Clivia. It is here that one will find the largest and handsomest specimens, whose shoots find their way to window-sills throughout the whole neighbourhood, just like Echinopses and fuchsias. Its great popularity was due not only to the pretty, white-spotted leaves and profuse flowers, but also to the great abundance of side shoots in the autumn from which the plant can easily be propagated. Today, *Aloe variegata* is a very popular ornamental and is propagated on a large scale in horticultural establishments.

It is cultivated with comparative ease in heavier, rich soil and in a spot with ample light; it does not tolerate direct sunlight and continual damp and cold, especially in winter when it is liable to lose its roots or perish altogether. It is propagated with ease from shoots, which quickly take root in sandy soil, or from the seed. Seedlings bear flowers within 2 to 3 years.

Plate 69

Agave victoriae reginae T. Moore

This cactus forms simple, usually stemless, broadly spherical rosettes about 50 to 70 cm across, with numerous, closely set leaves. These are angular, stiff, fleshy, erect, slightly curving towards the plant's centre, about 15 cm long, 7 cm wide at the base and tapering towards the tip. The colour is dark green with white stripes on the sides and edges that broaden towards the tip of the leaf. The end of the leaf terminates in two small and one strong, black-brown spines about 2 cm long. After many years it bears flowers on a 4 cm-high stalk.

Habitat: Northern Mexico, Nuevo Leon.

The specific name is in honour of Queen Victoria.

The genus *Agave* comprises approximately 300 species native to Mexico or Central America. In the main they are plants forming huge rosettes of stiff leaves, well-suited as ornamentals for parks or for collections in botanical gardens. They were introduced into Europe after the conquest of Mexico some time around 1521—1525. *Agave victoria reginae* is one of the loveliest of the small agaves and a showpiece of any small or large collection, besides being very well suited for cultivation in today's modern light and dry homes which the usual indoor plants do not tolerate well. It is propagated from the seed. It should be grown in nourishing, heavier soil and supplied with sufficient light and water during the growth period. In winter it should be kept at a temperature of 5° to 8°C.

Plate 70

Caralluma europaea (Guss.) N. E. Br.

Shrubs with branches 1 to 1.5 cm thick and 10 cm high, quadrilateral, blunt-toothed and strewn with greenish-brown flecks. The 10 or more flowers, are small and clustered at the tip of the shoot as a rule. They are five-pointed, 1 to 1.5 cm across, pale brown with brownish-red stripes.

Habitat: Island of Lampedusa in the Mediterranean, the east and west coast of West Africa all the way to the southern coast of Spain, which is the home of the variety *confusa*.

This very interesting plant is easy to grow. It does well in the dry, warm atmosphere, of today's modern apartments, together with other indoor plants both in the sunlight and in partial shade. Specimens grown in shade, however, flower irregularly and less profusely. The temperature of the room should be about 10° to 15°C, in summer it may be a great deal higher. The soil should be heavier and porous, though the plant will do well in any good soil with little humus. In winter it does not tolerate cold and damp. It is usually propagated from the seed, which is placed uncovered on the surface of damp, sandy soil. During the germination period the seed must not become too dry; it germinates within a few days at a temperature of 25°C. Propagation from shoots is the quickest; the cut surfaces must be left to dry in the sun for several days after which the shoots are put in pots filled with sandy soil, where they soon take root. Water is applied only after the shoots have developed roots.

Plate 71

Ceropegia sandersonii Decne

Ceropegia sandersonii has strong, creeping branches about 5 mm thick, often several metres long and coloured green. The leaves are thick, 3 to 5 cm long, green, heart-shaped, opposite (paired), on short stalks spaced 10 to 20 cm apart. The flowers on short stalks are pale green, swollen at the base, pentagonal at the top, up to 7 cm long and up to 4.5 cm across. When open the flower resembles a parachute, the edges of the apertures bordered with fine teeth with moving hairs. The top is coloured green with darker spots. The flowers emerge in the top part of the plant throughout the whole summer until late autumn.

Habitat: Natal.

Succulents comprise a great number of plants of such varied shapes that even the smallest collection will fascinate the uninitiated. The plants of the genus *Ceropegia* are no exception, even though they cannot rival such plants as *Euphorbia* or *Kalanchoe*, and are popular succulents grown in collections for their lantern-shaped flowers. They are generally semi-shrubs with fleshy branches, either drooping or creeping. The flowers are usually tubular, swollen at the base, with five petals often strewn with brightly coloured spots. This plant is cultivated, as a rule, in greenhouses or on window-sills between windows, where it has sufficient heat and moisture. *Ceropegia sandersonii* requires good, rich soil and a support for its creeping and twining branches. During the growing period water should be supplied in sufficient doses. The plant is propagated well from short shoots which quickly take root.

Ceropegia stapeliiformis Haw.

Short, gnarled stems, 1.5 to 2 cm thick, climbing or creeping, often burrowing into the ground. They are dull green, with grey-brown spots and white dots; later they taper towards the end and attain a height of up to 1.5 m. The leaves are small, pointed and greenish-brown. The flowers borne on short stalks in clusters of 2 to 4, are upright, about 6 cm long with a slender, slightly swollen tube, funnel-shaped at the mouth, white with brown spots on the outside, white and hairy on the inside.

Habitat: South Africa — Cape Province.

The specific name *stapeliiformis* means resembling the Stapelia.

Ceropegia stapeliiformis has either climbing stems, thin and more than one metre long, especially in the case of plants grown in a warm and moist atmosphere (greenhouses), or short, gnarled stems, about 20 cm long, creeping on the surface or burrowing into the ground. The flowers are the most fascinating examples to be found in the whole genus and even the buds have an interesting structure greatly resembling slender lanterns; on opening they form broad-limbed, funnel-shaped flowers with five narrow corolla lobes covered with white hairs. The fragile blooms last for several days on the plant.

Ceropegia stapeliiformis does well in greenhouses with other succulents, but it can also be grown on windowsills. During the growing period it requires heat, light and adequate watering, in winter light and a dry atmosphere with temperature of about 10°C. It is propagated from the seed but generally from part of the stem, which after drying is planted in the same type of soil as older plants, namely heavier, porous soil, where it quickly takes root.

Plate 73

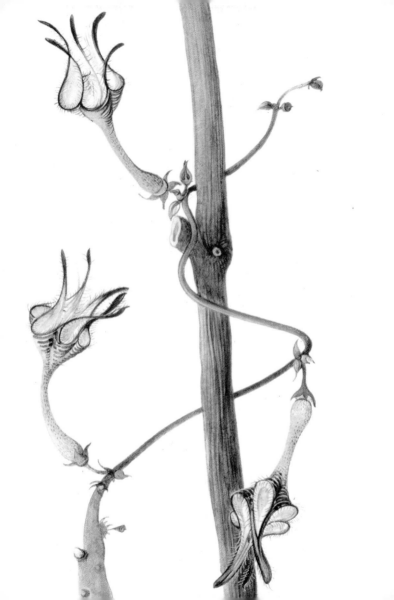

Conophytum pearsonii (L. Bol.) N. E. Br.

This plant forms clumps of stems 12 to 20 mm high and the same in width, broadly conical with flattened crown, smooth and bluish-green. The flowers emerge from a fissure about 3 mm long, are pale violet, glossy, and about 20 mm across. They arise at the beginning of the growing period in September to October.

Habitat: South Africa — Cape Province.

Conophytum pearsonii is one of the very succulent, caespitose plants which, next to Lithops, are among the most popular for their comparative ease of cultivation. Plants of the genus *Conophytum* are also known as "living pebbles". During the rest period (the summer months in Europe) a new body forms inside the old, gradually taking all the substances from it until all that remains is the skin, which dries and protects the young plant from the heat of the sun and excess evaporation of water. The resting *Conophytum* protected by this dry cover resembles a pebble and hence the name "living pebble".

Conophytum is less difficult to grow than Lithops. It does well in full sunlight, partial shade, greenhouses, hot-beds or houses. The growth period of most species is from August to March. The temperature should be about 10° to 12°C, the soil should be porous with slight humus and light application of water. During the rest period (from March till the end of July) water is withheld, with only light application to the soil in which the pots are placed, and the plant is provided with shade. The best method of propagation is by separating the clumps or planting seed. Seedlings are capable of bearing flowes within 2 to 3 years.

Cotyledon undulata Haw.

This plant grows singly or as bushes up to 50 cm high. The leaves are thick, fleshy, 8 to 12 cm long and 6 cm wide, oval, the edges wavy towards the tip with heavy chalky bloom. The flower stalk is 30 to 40 cm high, the flowers small, 2.5 cm long and golden-orange.

Habitat: South Africa — Cape Province.

The specific name *undulata* means wavy.

The genus *Cotyledon* has several very interesting species that are highly valued specimens in specialized collections, rarities that are considered true gems in the plant realm. Their place of origin, in the main, is Cape Province. They are usually low, very succulent shrubs with thick, short branches and small, generally deciduous leaves, e.g. *Cotyledon bucholziana, reticulata, pearsonii* and *ventricosa*. The last two are poisonous. A second group of the genus *Cotyledon*, more attractive in appearance, is distinguished by thick, larger leaves with a thick chalky bloom. The best known is *Cotyledon orbiculata*, which in its habitat forms shrubs 50 to 150 cm high. Also belonging to this group is the species *Cotyledon undulata* with its pretty variety *mucronata* which has smaller leaves with a reddish-brown margin. Well cultivated plants whose chalky bloom has not been rubbed off are truly beautiful and very delicate. When transplanting or transferring the plants from one spot to another, great care must be taken not to rub off this, their greatest ornament. Water, too, must not come in contact with the leaves and therefore the plant should not be sprinkled. *Cotyledon undulata* should be grown in a sunny, warm spot in heavy, clay soil. During the growing period it tolerates higher temperatures well. In winter it requires light and a dry atmosphere, temperature of 8° to 20°C. It is propagated from cuttings or from the leaves; from the seed only in large-scale propagation.

Crassula perforata Thunbg.

Crassula perforata forms smaller shrubs of prostrate, fleshy, later woody stems. The pairs of leaves are joined so that they appear to be like beads on a string. They are broadly ovate with short-pointed tip, at right angles to the stem, 1.5 to 2 cm long and 9 to 13 mm wide. The colour is grey-green with small whitish dots on the margin. The flowers emerge in spring — in April to May.

Habitat: South Africa — Cape Province.

The specific name *perforata* means perforated.

An entirely different group of *Crassula* are the pendant, shrub-like species assigned by A. Berger to the *Campanulatae*, group Perforata. One of the well-known and popular species of this group is *Crassula breviflora*, a small, delicate, shrub-like plant with thick, boat-shaped leaves edged with red.

Crassula perforata, also known as *perfossa*, is a popular succulent grown also as a suspended plant. In country homes one will find flower pots with the long, hanging branches on shelves or between windows. In the past years these modest plants have been gaining in popularity and a large number of hybrid species has been grown. These are less spreading, flower profusely and require the same treatment as *C. perforata*, which does well in light homes between the windows with adequate watering during the growing period. The soil should be heavier, porous and rich. In winter the plant needs light and only light application of water so that the leaves do not shrivel unduly. The best temperature is 7° to 10°C. It is propagated with ease from the short shoots which are potted into rich, porous soil where they quickly take root.

Echeveria pulvinata Rose

A low semi-shrub, 12 to 25 cm high, the leaves dark green, obovate with short pointed tip, 4 to 5 cm long, 2 to 4 cm wide and about 1 cm thick, with a dense coat of silvery white hairs. The leaves form a loose rosette, about 10 cm across. The short, semi-woody stem is covered at the top with white and at the base with brown hairs. The flower stalk, about 10 cm long, emerges between the leaves and bears several bright red flowers about 2 cm long with fleshy petals.

Habitat: Mexico — Oaxaca.

The specific name *pulvinata* means cushiony.

Echeveria pulvinata is a typical representative of the genus with very hairy leaves serving to prevent excessive evaporation as in the case of plants whose leaves are coated with wax. A popular species is *Echeveria leucotricha* with leaves about 8 cm long, fleshy, covered with white hairs, brownish at the tip and arranged in the form of a rosette. The flowers are red. An interesting species is *Echeveria setosa* which forms thick rosettes of long, dark green leaves with white hairs. The small red flowers with yellow tips grow in racemes. *Echeveria pulvinata* is a common, hardy species which can be grown well in the greenhouse, on the window-sill, or in a warm, sunny spot in the garden. In winter it requires light, a dry atmosphere and a temperature of 8° to 10°C. It is propagated from whole rosettes which may be planted directly in pots filled with sandy soil or, and this is the more frequent method, from leaf cuttings which are placed on sandy soil or peat.

Echeveria purpusorum Berg.

This plant forms rosettes about 10 cm across. The leaves are 3 to 4 cm long, oval, of triangular section, with short pointed tip, grey-green, finely dotted, and closely set. The flowers, 10 to 12 mm long, are carmine-red with yellow tips growing in racemes about 30 cm long. They emerge from May to June.

Habitat: Mexico.

Echeveria purpusorum is a species that is little cultivated even though it is the prettiest member of the whole genus. The shape of the thick, triangular, pointed leaves arranged in a compact rosette make this plant markedly different from the known Echeverias so that the name *Urbinia purpusii* that Dr. Rose originally gave it expresses this difference far better.

E. purpusorum is grown primarily in greenhouses, hotbeds, or window-cases. During the growing period it requires sufficient moisture and a warm and sunny spot, in winter light, a dry atmosphere and temperature of approximately 10°C. The soil should be heavier, rich and porous. It is propagated in spring or early summer from the seed, or more commonly from leaf cuttings which are placed on the surface of sandy soil or sandy peat where they soon take root, the small plants then being given the same treatment as seedlings. Larger plants are planted at the end of summer into small pots and given the same treatment as adult specimens.

Euphorbia grandicornis Goebel.

This plant forms thick, branched bushes comprising triangular, winged, pale green branches slanting upward from the stem. The edges are wavy with light brown border, which later turns dark brown. The thick, horn-shaped spines, arranged in pairs, are about 5 cm long, pale brown, later grey. The flowers are small and yellow, the fruit red.

Habitat: Africa — Natal, Tanganyika, Kenya.

Euphorbia grandicornis ranks among the most interesting of succulents. In greenhouses it grows to an imposing height of 1 to 2 m if given sufficient space, sun and water. It is equally well suited for cultivation in households or glassed porches. The long, thick spines are very dangerous and children in particular must be protected from them. When wounded all Euphorbias exude a white, poisonous milk that must not come in contact with the eye or an open wound. This characteristic of *Euphorbias* is the reason they are attacked by very few pests in the wild. Healthy, undamaged specimens are found and even in regions where there is a lack of pasture-land and water they are not molested by game.

Euphorbia grandicornis is generally cultivated in greenhouses, glassed verandahs or light, modern homes. It needs rich, heavier and porous soil and sufficient water in the growing period; in winter light, a dry atmosphere, and temperature of 10° to 15°C. It is propagated in spring from the seed or from 15 to 20 cm long cuttings, which after drying in a light, warm spot, i.e. after about 20 days, are planted in sandy soil where they soon take root. They are then given the same treatment as adult plants.

Plate 79

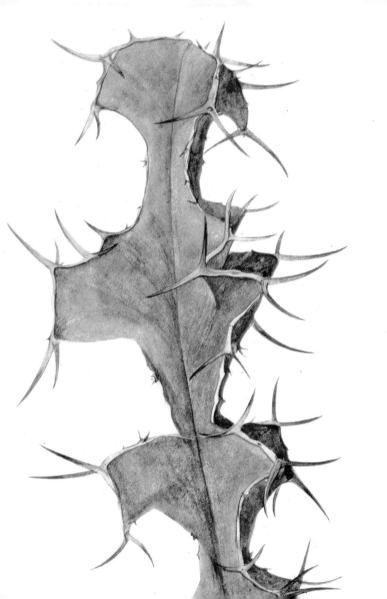

Euphorbia horrida Boiss.

Spherical in youth, 10 to 15 cm across, the plant becomes columnar in age, up to 1 m in height, makes side shoots freely at the base and grows in clusters. The skin is dark green with grey tinge, corky brown at the base. The ribs, 12 or more, are narrow with toothed edges and three, 1 to 2 cm long, thorns set 1 to 2 cm apart. *Euphorbia horrida* is a dioecious plant, the flowers are nondescript, the fruit is a triloculate capsule.

Habitat: South Africa — Cape Province.

The specific name *horrida* means frightening.

Euphorbia horrida is a very succulent plant greatly resembling a very spiny cactus. It is highly prized by growers specializing in succulents, in the same way as *Euphorbia obesa*, *E. bupleurifolia* and *E. fasciculata*. In its native land it is used as a host plant for the parasitic mistletoe *(Viscum album)*, the seeds of which are pressed into the grooves between the ribs where they soon germinate and penetrate into the plant tissue. Small shoots and leaves often appear even in the second year. The flowers and fruits are a bright red.

Euphorbia horrida is not difficult to grow if at least the minimum requirements of the species are respected. In summer it needs sufficient sun, heat and careful application of water; in winter adequate light, a temperature of 10° to 15°C and a dry atmosphere. The soil should be porous, heavier and nourishing. It is usually propagated from shoots or from the seed, which has comparatively poor powers of germination.

Plate 80

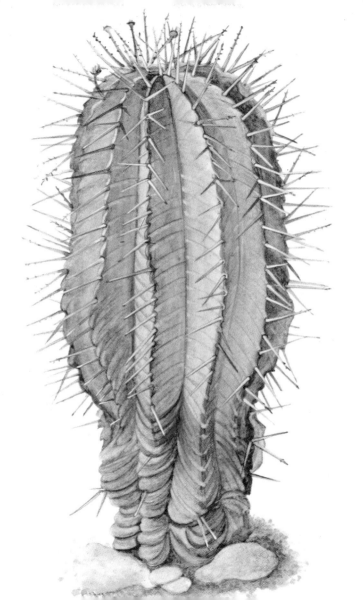

Euphorbia obesa Hook. f.

The body is spherical to slightly columnar, the crown slightly depressed, diameter 8 to 10 cm, height 12 cm or more. The colour is pale to dark green, brownish-green with reddish-brown horizontal stripes in the sun. The ribs are broad and flat with many small tubercles on the edge. Older and imported plants have brown corky spots at the base. The flowers are small and nondescript, with one plant bearing all staminate or all pistillate blooms. The ovary is triloculate, dehiscing at maturity and catapulting the fairly large seeds to a distance of up to one metre.

Habitat: South Africa — Cape Province.

The specific name *obesa* means fat.

The first specimens of this plant were sent to England in 1897 to the botanical gardens at Kew under the name *Euphorbia meloformis*. There they were classified by Prof. Hooker and in 1903 described as the new species *Euphorbia obesa*. The imports all died and it was not until attempts to cultivate better adapted young plants from the seed had succeeded that the species ceased being such a great rarity. Today it is fairly widespread and is far easier to grow than was the case some years ago. Best suited for the purpose are low vessels, bowls, heavier, porous, clay soil with a larger portion of crushed brick and warm sunny site. Water is supplied lightly, only when the soil is dry. In winter *Euphorbia obesa* should be placed in a dry, light spot where the temperature does not drop below 12°C. It is propagated only from the seed, attaining maturity after three or four years.

Plate 81

Faucaria lupina (Haw.) Schwant.

In youth it grows singly, later forming clumps about 15 cm across with a short stem. The leaves are an intense green, about 4 cm long, 1.5 cm wide, triangular. The inner or upper part of the leaf is flat, the outer or lower part keel-shaped with blunt tip. The upper edges have long, fine teeth curved towards the centre of the plant. The flowers emerge in the centre of the plant, are yellow and measure about 3.5 cm in diameter.

Habitat: South Africa — Cape Province.

The specific name *lupina* means wolf's.

Faucaria is an old and well-known member of the *mesembryanthemum* group. These are popular plants not only for the ease with which they are grown, but also for the rewarding flower-bearing properties. The growing period is during the summer and is fairly short. The flowers arise at the end of summer and last until autumn if the weather is warm and sunny. The various species differ very little. The only one that can be determined with certainty is *Faucaria tuberculata* which has short, thick leaves strewn with warts on the upper side. The flowers, about 4 cm across, are yellow. *Faucaria bosscheana* and the variety *haagei* have leaves with a different structure and with white margins. *Faucaria tigrina* has thick leaves with delicate pale spots on the upper side and densely, fine-toothed edges. The remaining species are more or less alike.

Faucarias are easy to grow. In summer, during the growth period, they require sun, warmth and fresh air with adequate watering; during the rest period light, sufficient fresh air; in winter a dry atmosphere. *Faucaria lupina* is also well suited for cultivation in a sunny household situation. It is propagated by dividing the clumps or from the seed. The seedlings bear flowers in two to three years.

Plate 82

Fenestraria rhopalophylla N. E. Br.

A rosette of long, thin cylindrical leaves, later forming clumps about 10 cm across. The leaves are pale green, club-shaped at the tip, 0.5 to 1 cm thick, about 5 cm long terminating in a convex, almost circular, green, transparent "window". The flowers, pure white and about 5 cm across, are borne on 5 cm long stalks.

Habitat: South Africa — Cape Province.

The specific name *rhopalophylla* means with club-shaped leaves.

The genus *Fenestraria* (window plants) erected by N. E. Brown, is very aptly named. The "window" leaves serve to disperse the sun's rays on to the tissues containing chlorophyll, located along the margin of the leaf. This is a very interesting genus both from the biological and morphological aspects. In its habitat the greater part of the plant is underground with only the leaf tips with their translucent panes emerging above the surface. It is thus that *Fenestrarias* protect themselves against the sun's heat, excessive evaporation and pests.

Fenestraria species, though not difficult to cultivate, require green fingers. They are very sensitive to damp and must be watered with great care even during the growth period. They need good, porous soil (leaf-mould or old hotbed soil) with crushed brick or stone in the roportion of one part soil to two parts crushed brick. During the growing period they require much light and heat: in winter light, a dry atmosphere and temperature of 10° to 15°C. It is propagated well from the seed which germinates readily. The seedlings are sensitive and do not tolerate permanent damp. They mature within two or three years.

Frithia pulchra N. E. Br.

Small rosettes of nine or more, dark green leaves, about 3.5 cm long, round with shallow longitudinal groove and flat top. The tips are formed by an irregularly oval, translucent, pale-green "window", 0.5 to 0.8 cm across. The flowers arise in the centre of the plant, unlike Fenestraria where they emerge on the side. They are about 2 cm across and carmine-red with white centre.

Habitat: Transvaal.

The specific name *pulchra* means beautiful.

"Window" plants include besides the genus *Frithia* and *Fenestraria*, *Lithops*, *Ophthalmophyllum*, *Haworthia truncata*, *H. maughanii* and others. They are all very interesting plants and very scarce. In their habitat they grow underground with only the tips of the leaves emerging above the surface so that they are difficult to find. On the other hand, however, this is excellent protection against pests.

In cultures they are planted in small flower pots in porous soil (leaf-mould or old hotbed soil plus crushed brick) with the leaves above the surface. The pots are placed in sand or crushed brick; during the growing period, i.e. from March to May, water is applied to the material between the pots so that the moisture reaches the roots by seeping through. *Frithia pulchra* is a fairly hardy plant requiring a light location, in winter a dry atmosphere, light and temperature of 10° to 12°C. It is propagated only from the seed which has good powers of germination. The seedlings are sensitive and do not tolerate permanent damp and cold. They mature and bear flowers in two to three years.

Plate 84

Gasteria armstrongii   Schoenl.

This species is a miniature plant generally less than 10 cm in size. The thick, leathery leaves are tongue-shaped. They are dark green and strewn with small warts. New leaves are erect at first, later appressed to the older leaves which grow horizontally. The flowers are fairly small, pink and arranged in a loose raceme 30 cm long.

Habitat: South Africa — Cape Province.

Gasteria armstrongii is a favourite succulent because of its ease of cultivation, hardiness and small dimensions which make it well suited for small collections. The plant was discovered by W. Armstrong, after whom the species is named and who, in 1912, sent seeds to the botanical garden in Vienna from which twelve plants were grown. From there the plant spread to other botanical gardens and private collections.

It is cultivated like all Gasterias in fairly heavy soil rich in humus, in the shade. Direct sunlight and permanent lack of water weaken the plant excessively. This species is well suited for cultivation on window-sills in cities together with other ornamentals. It can be propagated from the seed, but usually from the shoots made by older plants.

Plate 85

Gasteria maculata (Thunbg.) Haw.

The leaves of this plant are arranged in two rows, often spirally. They are stiff, thick, about 20 cm long and 5 cm wide. The surface is flat or slightly convex, glossy with white spots that are pinkish in the sun. The flowers are arranged in a loose raceme about 30 cm long. The individual flowers are tubular, swollen at the base, red with green border. They appear several times during the year.

Habitat: South Africa — Cape Province.

The specific name *maculata* means spotted.

All species of *Gasteria* are hardy, easy-to-grow plants, well suited for dry, modern homes. They will thrive, however, in any spot where there is adequate light, even a northern exposure, but direct sunlight is not tolerated well. Many species are very similar and hybridization is quite common, which causes great difficulty in their precise identification. *Gasteria maculata* is a popular species cultivated in houses in a shady spot in rich heavy soil. The first flowers begin to emerge in early spring. Summer is a brief rest period when water is applied sparingly, just enough to keep the plant from becoming too dry, liberal application being resumed again in August. In winter, water is withheld as long as the temperature does not rise above 10°C. The plant is generally propagated from leaf cuttings or shoots, less frequently from the seed because of the ease of hybridization with other species. The seeds are large, almost black, and are planted in sandy soil where they germinate fairly quickly.

Plate 86

Haworthia cymbiformis (Haw.) Duv.

Forms rosettes of pale green, very thick leaves, 7 to 10 cm across, making shoots freely at the base so that they form large clumps. The leaves are fleshy, boat-shaped, about 4 cm long, 2.5 cm wide, with pale, faintly striped "windows" on the upper side. The roots are pale, fleshy and break easily. The flower stalk is about 30 cm long, the flowers are small and white. They emerge several times a year.

Habitat: South Africa — Cape Province.

The specific name *cymbiformis* means boat-shaped.

Haworthia cymbiformis belongs to the large group of plants with pale green, soft-fleshed leaves with transparent, elongate spots ("window" plants). Other well-known species of this group are *H. bilineata*, *H. cuspidata*, *H. lepida*, *H. optusa*, *H. planifolia*, *H. retusa*, *H. ryderiana* and *H. turgida*. Although these species belong to different systematic groups their cultivation is the same. *Haworthia cymbiformis* thrives on window-sills in partial shade; it does not tolerate direct sunlight. During the growth period, which begins in early spring, the plants require warmth and sufficient moisture. During the summer rest period and in winter, water is applied sparingly, purely to prevent the plants drying up. They do well in heavier, nourishing and porous soil. In winter they need light and a temperature of 8° to 10°C. Propagation is from shoots, which do well, but rarely from the seed and then only if it is certain that it is a pure strain.

Haworthia fasciata (Willd.) Haw.

Forms rosettes of leaves about 8 cm across, forming whole groups of rosettes in age. The leaves are glossy, green, 4 to 6 cm long, about 13 mm wide, triangular and flat on the upper side. The underside is convex with large white warts arranged in horizontal rows. The flowers are small, whitish arranged in an upright raceme about 30 to 40 cm high. They emerge several times in the year.

Habitat: South Africa — Cape Province.

The specific name *fasciata* means banded.

The genus *Haworthia* was so named in honour of the British scientist and collector of succulents Adrian Hardy Haworth, who described many plants.

Haworthia fasciata with its varieties and forms is one of the basic plants of any collection. It is widely cultivated not only by growers of cacti and succulents but also by flower lovers, mainly youngsters, for its ease of cultivation. It does well almost everywhere — in the greenhouse, hotbed and on the window-sill. However, it does not tolerate direct sunlight or a dry atmosphere during the growth period, the latter being the cause of the leaf tips drying. The growing period lasts from March till May, followed by the summer rest period till the end of August. At this time water is applied lightly, only so the plants do not become too dry. September marks the beginning of a new growth period. In winter water is applied lightly and occasionally, so that the plants do not become too dry, and the temperature should be between 6° and 10°C. Propagation is easy from the rosettes, which arise at the base of older plants. Propagation from the seed is employed only when purity of the species is assured, for Haworthias hybridize easily.

246   *Plate 88*

Haworthia tesselata   Haw.

Rosettes of spirally arranged, fleshy leaves, 6 to 10 cm
across. The leaves are stiff, fleshy, dark green, 4 to 5 cm
long, 2 to 5 cm wide, triangular. The leaf surface is often
flat, glossy, translucent, with 5 to 7 longitudinal lines
branching to form a network, and coloured dark
brownish-green in the sun. The flowers grow in loose
racemes up to 30 cm long; they are small and whitish-
green and arise several times throughout the year.

Habitat. South Africa — Cape Province.

The specific name *tesselata* means net-like.

Haworthia tesselata has several handsome varieties
(scientific literature lists 17, including forms) found only
in specialized collections. It is a small and hardy plant
distinguished by the colour and shape of its leaves, which
look bronze in the sun. It occurs amongst other succulents and does well in spots protected from direct sunlight. Being small, it is well suited for cultivation in the
household. In summer it has a short rest period when
growth is arrested; at this time it must not be watered,
for otherwise it loses its roots and the plant might rot.

It is cultivated in heavy, porous and nourishing soil
in partial shade, at a temperature between 5° to 20°C.In
winter it requires a dry atmosphere and temperature of
5° to 7° C. Propagation is usually from shoots or from
the seed. Seedlings attain maturity within three years.

Haworthia truncata Schoenl.

Haworthia truncata is a small, low succulent plant about 6 cm in diameter. It consists of two rows of thick, dark green leaves about 4 cm long, with truncated tip and irregularly oval, almost transparent spot. The flowers arise in the centre of the plant. They are small, whitish and grow in a loose raceme 20 to 30 cm long.

Habitat: South Africa — Cape Province.

The specific name *truncata* means truncated.

Haworthia truncata is one of the most interesting of the succulents. In South Africa, especially in the desert region, where the temperature of the ground ranges from 50° to 60°C and where there is a great dearth of water, a large number of odd succulents occur. Some, besides being equipped with thick leaves, have a special protective device against the intense solar radiation. This is a sort of "window", found at the tip of each leaf in *Haworthica truncata*. It serves to let through only a certain amount of the sun's rays necessary for assimilation, in the same way as in *Lithops* and *Fenestraria*. In its habitat, i.e. in Africa, *Haworthia truncata* is buried in the ground up to the transparent leaf tips, thus protecting itself against excessive evaporation. Dr. K. von Poelnitz determined further the forms *crassa, normalis* and *tenuis*, differing from the type in the shape and size of the "window". These, however, are not often found in collections. Its remarkable shape and small size make *Haworthia truncata* a great favourite, though it is a scarce species. Its cultivation requires no special treatment. It should be grown in heavier, porous soil and partial shade. Water should be applied with care during the growth period and practically withheld during the summer rest period; watering is resumed again in autumn. In winter the plant needs light, a dry atmosphere and temperature of about 10°C. It is propagated from the seed.

Kalanchoë tomentosa Baker

This plant forms shrubs up to 50 cm high, branching at the base. The leaves and stems are thickly covered with short, white hairs. The leaves are narrow, oval, about 7 cm long and 2 cm wide, with blunt tip. The tips of young leaves are toothed, the margins stained with brown.

Habitat: Madagascar.

The specific name *tomentosa* means covered with matted hairs.

The genus *Kalanchoë* is very large and not all the species are suitable for cultivation in collections. They were divided by H. Jacobsen into three sections, *Kalanchoë tomentosa* belonging to the third, which comprises many well-known species grown as ornamentals. One such species — *Kalanchoë beharensis* of Madagascar — is an interesting succulent with large, wavy, arrow-shaped leaves, 20 cm long, thickly covered with dark brown hairs on the upper side and pale ones on the underside. *Kalanchoë orgyalis*, also of Madagascar, is popular with collectors as well. The ovate leaves, 7 cm long and 4 cm wide, are covered with short, bronze-brown hairs on the upper side and pale ones on the underside. *Kalanchoë marmorata* of Eritrea and Ethiopia has oval, red-spotted leaves with toothed margin and smooth surface devoid of hairs.

Kalanchoë tomentosa is cultivated for its ornamental, hairy leaves. It also does well on window-sills in a sunny spot. In winter it requires light, a dry atmosphere and temperature of 7° to 10°C. It is propagated from cuttings, which are planted in heavy, porous soil, or from the leaves which are placed in a dish of sandy soil.

Plate 91

Lithops aucampiae L. Bol.

The stems of this striking plant are broad, measuring more in width than in height, 3 cm and 2 cm respectively. The reddish-brown upper part is slightly convex, divided by a shallow slit into two unequal halves with red network pattern. Near the slit are dark green, translucent "windows". The flowers are yellow, about 2.5 cm across, emerging in the early autumn.

Habitat: Transvaal.

Lithops aucampiae is a striking, reddish brown plant pressed close to the ground, its stems closely resembling pebbles. Prof. K. Dinter described them as mimicry plants which, just like some animals, are adapted to their surroundings both in shape and colour. They are very succulent, usually with one or more pairs of joined, fleshy leaves. They grow in dry, desert regions, their whole bodies except for the crown concealed in sand or gravel which protects them from the heat of the sun. The plant surface of Lithops has no green colouring matter. The shape and coloration serve to reflect and disperse most of the sun's rays, permitting absorption of only such a quantity as is necessary for the plant's life processes. This energy is transmitted by a clear fluid to the layer of chlorophyll grains located along the edge of the plant body. It is here, underground, that the process of assimilation takes place.

Lithops aucampiae needs direct sunlight, adequate heat during the growing period and careful application of water. In winter it requires light, a dry atmosphere, and temperature of 10° to 12°C. It is propagated from the seed; seedlings bear flowers within two to three years.

Plate 92

Lithops volkii Schw. ex Jacobsen

The body is caespitose with 2 to 4 stems to a clump, up to 4 cm high, grey-blue, sometimes with a reddish tinge. The leaves, slightly convex at the tip, are about 3 cm across, grey-blue with a whitish tinge, divided by a shallow groove into two unequal halves and covered with red dots which often merge to form lines. Some plants are without markings and have only a number of pale, almost transparent spots. The flowers are 2.5 cm across and an intense yellow, arising as early as July.

Habitat: South-west Africa.

Lithops volkii is a comparative newcomer to collections. It is one of the 75 known, popular "living pebbles". In its habitat it grows on mounds in quartz gravel so that it is difficult to distinguish from its surroundings, thus fully substantiating the description of Lithops as mimicry plants. The growing period of *Lithops volkii* is from April to September and cultivation is the same as with other species of this genus. *Lithops volkii*, however, is not as sensitive to possible excess application of water or its omission. In the case of such very succulent plants it is recommended that the flowerpots be placed in a box filled with crushed brick, sand, peat with sand or the like and that this be watered. Lithops are grown in soil comprising two parts crushed brick and one part light, sandy soil (leaf-mould or old hotbed soil), in direct sunlight, at a temperature of up to 50°C in summer. In winter it requires light, a dry atmosphere and temperature of 10° to 15°C. It is propagated best from the seed, which germinates within one or two weeks in a warm and moist atmosphere. The seeds are placed in flowerpots in light sandy soil. Seedlings are very delicate in the first year.

Plate 93

Sedum adolphii Hamet

A low semi-shrub with fleshy or semi-woody branches, more or less erect. The leaves are very fleshy, 3.5 cm long, 1.5 cm wide, ovate, pale green, those at the end of the branch growing in a compact cluster.

Habitat: Mexico.

The genus *Sedum* is very widespread, some species being native to Europe; a large number occur in the regions bordering the Mediterranean. They also grow in East Asia, Central Africa, Madagascar, South America, western and south-western United States and Mexico. Occurring in the wild are one- and two-year species as well as permanent succulent shrubs that are either erect or prostrate. Besides *Sedum adolphii* many other species, chiefly Mexican, are cultivated as household plants or succulents. These include: *Sedum allantoides* — a low, 20 to 30 cm high, small shrub with whitish-green, fat, keel-shaped leaves, *Sedum nutans* with lanceolate, brown-green leaves forming a rosette 10 cm or more in diameter, *Sedum nussbaumerianum* with lanceolate, yellowish-green leaves bordered red, and the striking *Sedum pachyphyllum* with keel-shaped, fresh green, red-tipped leaves. All these species are popular succulents, well suited for cultivation in the household or in a sunny spot in the garden in summer. In winter they require light, a dry atmosphere and temperature of about 5° to 8°C. They can be successfully propagated from cuttings, which are planted immediately in quite heavy, porous soil, or from the leaves, which are placed in dishes or pots on sandy soil where they soon take root, the small plants being subsequently planted in small flowerpots.

Stapelia grandiflora Mass.

This plant forms clumps of quadrangular stems up to 30 cm high, 3 to 4 cm thick, intense green, convex, and covered with fine hairs. The edges of the stems are compressed and toothed. The pointed, swollen pink buds emerge at the base of a new shoot on short stalks, always several in a group. The corolla lobes are triangular, purple, horizontally striped, and thickly covered with soft, grey hairs.

Habitat: South Africa — Cape Province.

The specific name *grandiflora* means large-flowered.

Stapelia grandiflora attracts even the uninitiated by the structure and size of its flowers, which are among the largest in the whole genus. All species of *Stapelia* are interesting, unusual succulents, cultivated by specialists along with *Caralluma, Trichocaulon, Hoodia, Huernia, Piaranthus,* etc.

Stapelia grandiflora is easy to cultivate. It grows just as well in a sunny spot as in partial shade in the greenhouse, hotbed or on the window-sill. Each stem bears five or six purple flowers a year. These are up to 15 cm in diameter and have an unpleasant odour. Stapelias should be planted in low flower-pots or bowls filled with porous, clay soil. They are propagated from shoots which are left to dry in the sun for several days and then planted in sandy soil where they quickly take root, at which stage water is applied. The plants can also be propagated from the seed which germinates in two to three days in a warm and moist atmosphere. The seedlings are delicate.

Stapelia variegata L.

This plant forms thick clumps of short stems, about 10 cm long, coloured green to grey-green, often reddish in the sun, with narrow, erect teeth. The buds, one to five in number arise at the base of new shoots; they are pale green, swollen and borne on short stalks. The open flower is flat, fleshy, 5 to 8 cm across, wrinkled, dull yellow inside with dark brown spots scattered over the surface or arranged in irregular rows. Inside the flower is a thick somewhat rounded ring, coloured dull yellow with small brown spots. The corolla lobes are broadly ovate, bending back in time. Like *S. grandiflora,* the odour is that of rotting meat.

Habitat: South Africa — Cape Province.

The specific name *variegata* means variegated.

Specialized collections contain many varieties differing from one another in coloration and also in the size and arrangement of the spots on the flowers. *Stapelia variegata* is one of the succulents that grows well under many kinds of treatment. It does just as well in heavy clay soil as in light sandy leaf-mould, in the sun as in partial shade. It is popular for the easy and rapid propagation from the shoots and for its flowering properties, the blooms emerging throughout the summer until late autumn. In winter it requires light, the sparing application of water — only enough to keep the shoots from becoming too dry, and a temperature of 7° to 10°C. It is propagated from the shoots, which are planted in flower-pots as soon as they have dried, and also from the seed, but the latter only if it is certain that it is a pure strain.

Index

Aporocactus flagelliformis 72
Astrophytum asterias 74
Astrophytum capricorne 76
Astrophytum myriostigma 78
Astrophytum ornatum 80
Aylostera kupperiana 82
Aztekium ritteri 84
Brasilicactus graessneri 86
Brasilicactus haselbergii 88
Cephalocereus senilis 90
Cleistocactus baumannii
    var. flavispinus 92
Chamaecereus silvestrii 94
Copiapoa montana 96
Dolichothele longimamma 98
Echinocactus grusonii 100
Echinocereus pectinatus 102
Echinocereus pulchellus 104
Echinofossulocactus
    pentacanthus 106
Echinopsis eyriesii 108
Epithelantha micromeris 110
Eriocactus leninghausii 112
Eriocereus martinii 114
Eriosyce ceratistes 116
Espostoa lanata 118
Gymnocalycium
    baldianum 120
Gymnocalycium
    denudatum 122

Gymnocalycium den.
    cv. J. Šuba 124
Gymnocalycium gibbosum 126
Gymnocalycium
    friedrichii 128
Gymnocalycium
    multiflorum 130
Gymnocalycium
    quehlianum 132
Haematocactus
    setispinus 134
Islaya flavida 136
Leuchtenbergia principis 138
Lobivia famatimensis 140
Lobivia jajoiana 142
Lobivia wrightiana 144
Lophophora williamsii 146
Mamillaria applanata 148
Mamillaria bocasana 150
Mamillaria bombycina 152
Mamillaria centricirrha 154
Mamillaria hahniana 156
Mamillaria sheldonii 158
Mamillaria zeilmanniana 160
Mediolobivia aureiflora· 162
Mediolobivia ritteri 164
Neochilenia jussieuii 166
Notocactus concinnus 168
Obregonia denegrii 170
Opuntia microdasys 172

Oreocereus neocelsianus	174	Conophytum pearsonii	218
Parodia chrysacanthion	176	Cotyledon undulata	220
Parodia mutabilis	178	Crassula perforata	222
Parodia nivosa	180	Echeveria pulvinata	224
Parodia sanguiniflora	182	Echeveria purpusorum	226
Pilosocereus palmeri	184	Euphorbia grandicornis	228
Phyllocactus hybridus	186	Euphorbia horrida	230
Pseudolobivia aurea	188	Euphorbia obesa	232
Pseudolobivia kermesina	190	Faucaria lupina	234
Rebutia marsoneri	192	Fenestraria	
Rebutia senilis	194	rhopalophylla	236
Strombocactus disciformis	196	Frithia pulchra	238
Thelocactus bicolor	198	Gasteria armstrongii	240
Trichocereus candicans	200	Gasteria maculata	242
Turbinicarpus		Haworthia cymbiformis	244
lophophoroides	202	Haworthia fasciata	246
Zygocactus truncatus	204	Haworthia tesselata	248
		Haworthia truncata	250
Aloe concinna	206	Kalanchoë tomentosa	252
Aloe variegata	208	Lithops aucampiae	254
Agave victoriae reginaea	210	Lithops volkii	256
Caralluma europea	212	Sedum adolphii	258
Ceropegia sandersonii	214	Stapelia grandiflora	260
Ceropegia stapeliiformis	216	Stapelia variegata	262